POEMS

Selected Poems

The Gulf

Another Life

Sea Grapes

The Star-Apple Kingdom

The Fortunate Traveller

Midsummer

Collected Poems: 1948–1984

The Arkansas Testament

Omeros

The Bounty

PLAYS

Dream on Monkey Mountain and Other Plays

The Joker of Seville and O Babylon!

Remembrance and Pantomime

Three Plays: The Last Carnival; Beef, No Chicken;

A Branch of the Blue Nile

The Odyssey

ESSAYS

What the Twilight Says

TIEPOLO'S HOUND

DEREK WALCOTT

FARRAR, STRAUS AND GIROUX

NEW YORK

Farrar, Straus and Giroux
19 Union Square West, New York 10003

Copyright © 2000 by Derek Walcott
Distributed in Canada by Douglas & McIntyre Ltd.
Printed in the United States of America
First edition, 2000

Library of Congress Cataloging-in-Publication Data
Walcott, Derek.
    Tiepolo's hound / Derek Walcott.—1st ed.
        p.   cm.
    ISBN 0-374-10587-1 (alk. paper)
        1. West Indians—Travel—Europe—Poetry.   2. Pissarro, Camille, 1830–1903
    —Poetry.   3. Quests (Expeditions)—Poetry.   4. Painters—France—Poetry.
    5. Painting—Poetry.   I. Title.
    PR9272.9.W3 T54 2000
    811—dc21   99-051762

We gratefully acknowledge the photographs of
Seth Rubin, New York; Chester Williams, St. Lucia;
and Cyan Studios, Trinidad.

For Sigrid

BOOK ONE

1

They stroll on Sundays down Dronningens Street,
passing the bank and the small island shops

quiet as drawings, keeping from the heat
through Danish arches until the street stops

at the blue, gusting harbour, where like commas
in a shop ledger gulls tick the lined waves.

Sea-light on the cod barrels writes: *St. Thomas*,
the salt breeze brings the sound of Mission slaves

chanting deliverance from all their sins
in tidal couplets of lament and answer,

the horizon underlines their origins—
Pissarros from the ghetto of Braganza

who fled the white hoods of the Inquisition
for the bay's whitecaps, for the folding cross

of a white herring gull over the Mission
droning its passages from Exodus.

Before the family warehouse, near the Customs,
his uncle jerks the locks, rattling their chains,

and lifts his beard to where morning comes
across wide water to the Gentile mountains.

Out of the cobalt bay, her blunt bow cleaving
the rising swell that racing bitterns skip,

the mail boat moans. They feel their bodies leaving
the gliding island, not the blowing ship.

A mongrel follows them, black as its shadow,
nosing their shadows, scuttling when the bells

exult with pardon. Young Camille Pissarro
studies the schooners in their stagnant smells.

He and his starched Sephardic family,
followed from a nervous distance by the hound,

retrace their stroll through Charlotte Amalie
in silence as its Christian bells resound,

sprinkling the cobbles of Dronningens Gade,
the shops whose jalousies in blessing close,

through repetitions of the oval shade
of Danish arches to their high wooden house.

The Synagogue of Blessing and Peace and Loving Deeds
is shut for this Sabbath. The mongrel cowers

through a park's railing. The bells recede.
The afternoon is marked by cedar flowers.

Their street of letters fades, this page of print
in the bleached light of last century recalls

with the sharp memory of a mezzotint:
days of cane carts, the palms' high parasols.

2

My wooden window frames the Sunday street
which a black dog crosses into Woodford Square.

From a stone church, tribal voices repeat
the tidal couplets of lament and prayer.

Behind the rusted lances of a railing
stands the green ribbed fan of a Traveller's Tree;

an iron gate, its croton hedge availing
itself of every hue, screeches on entry.

Walk down the path, enter the yawning stone,
its walls as bare as any synagogue

of painted images. The black congregation
frown in the sun at the sepulchral dog.

There was a *shul* in old-time Port of Spain,
but where its site precisely was is lost

in the sunlit net of maps whose lanes contain
a spectral faith, white as the mongrel's ghost.

Stiller the palms on Sunday, fiercer the grass,
blacker the shade under the boiling trees,

sharper the shadows, quieter the grace
of afternoon, the city's emptiness.

And over the low hills there is the haze
of heat and a smell of rain in the noise

of trees lightly thrashing where one drop has
singed the scorched asphalt as more petals rise.

A silent city, blest with emptiness
like an engraving. Ornate fretwork eaves,

and the heat rising from the pitch in wires,
from empty back yards with calm breadfruit leaves,

their walls plastered with silence, the same streets
with the same sharp shadows, laced verandahs closed

in torpor, until afternoon repeats
the long light with its croton-coloured crowds

in the Savannah, not the Tuileries, but
still the Rock Gardens' brush-point cypresses

like a Pissarro canvas, past the shut
gate of the President's Palace, flecked dresses

with gull cries, white flowers and cricketers,
coconut carts, a frilled child with the hoop

of the last century, and, just as it was
in Charlotte Amalie, a slowly creaking sloop.

Laventille's speckled roofs, just as it was
in Cazabon's day, the great Savannah cedars,

the silent lanes at sunrise, parked cars
quiet at their culverts, trainers, owners, breeders

before they moved the paddocks, the low roofs
under the low hills, the sun-sleeved Savannah

under the elegance of grass-muffled hooves,
the cantering snort, the necks reined in; a

joy that was all smell, fresh dung; the jokes
of the Indian grooms, that civilising

culture of horses, the *fin de siècle* spokes
of trotting carriages, and egrets rising,

as across olive hills a flock of pigeons,
keeping its wide ellipse over dark trees

to the Five Islands, soundlessly joins
its white flecks to the sails on quiet seas.

The white line of chalk birds draws on an Asia
of white-lime walls, prayer flags, and minarets,

blackbirds bring Guinea to thorns of acacia,
and in the saffron of Tiepolo sunsets,

the turbulent paradise of bright rotundas
over aisles of cane, and censer-carried mists,

then, blazing from the ridges of Maracas—
the croton hues of the Impressionists.

3

On my first trip to the Modern I turned a corner,
rooted before the ridged linen of a Cézanne.

A still life. I thought how clean his brushes were!
Across that distance light was my first lesson.

I remember stairs in couplets. The Metropolitan's
marble authority, I remember being

stunned as I studied the exact expanse
of a Renaissance feast, the art of seeing.

Then I caught a slash of pink on the inner thigh
of a white hound entering the cave of a table,

so exact in its lucency at *The Feast of Levi*,
I felt my heart halt. Nothing, not the babble

of the unheard roar that rose from the rich
pearl-lights embroidered on ballooning sleeves,

sharp beards, and gaping goblets, matched the bitch
nosing a forest of hose. So a miracle leaves

its frame, and one epiphanic detail
illuminates an entire epoch:

a medal by Holbein, a Vermeer earring, every scale
of a walking mackerel by Bosch, their sacred shock.

Between me and Venice the thigh of a hound;
my awe of the ordinary, because even as I write,

paused on a step of this couplet, I have never found
its image again, a hound in astounding light.

Everything blurs. Even its painter. Veronese
or Tiepolo in a turmoil of gesturing flesh,

drapery, columns, arches, a crowded terrace,
a balustrade with leaning figures. In the mesh

of Venetian light on its pillared arches
Paolo Veronese's *Feast in the House of Levi*

opens on a soundless page, but no shaft catches
my memory: one stroke for a dog's thigh!

4

But isn't that the exact perspective of loss,
that the loved one's features blur, in dimming detail,

the smile with its dimpled corners, her teasing voice
rasping with affection, as Time draws its veil,

until all you remember are her young knees
gleaming from an olive dress, her way of walking,

as if on a page of self-arranging trees,
hair a gold knot, rose petals silently talking?

I catch an emerald sleeve, light knits her hair,
in a garland of sculpted braids, her burnt cheeks;

catch her sweet breath, be the blest one near her
at that Lucullan table, lean when she speaks,

as clouds of centuries pass over the brilliant ground
of the fresco's meats and linen, while her wrist

in my forced memory caresses an arched hound,
as all its figures melt in the fresco's mist.

II

1

What should be true of the remembered life
is a freshness of detail: this is how it was—

the almond's smell from a torn almond leaf,
the spray glazing your face from the bursting waves.

And I, walking like him around the wharf's
barrels and schooners, felt a steady love

growing in me, plaited with the strong weaves
of a fish pot, watching its black hands move,

saw in the shadows in which it believes,
in ruined lanes, and rusted roofs above

the lanes, a language, light, and the dark lives
in sour doorways, an alighting dove.

Our street of smoke and fences, gutters gorged
with weed and reeking, scorching iron grooves

of rusted galvanise, a dialect forged
from burning asphalt, and a sky that moves

with thunderhead cumuli grumbling with rain,
and mongrels staggering to cross the pitch

under the olive Morne that held the ruin
of the barracks, yet all was privilege;

especially if, across the harbour, noon
struck its ring of waves, and the ochre walls

of the old cantonment in the still lagoon
reflected their Italian parallels.

Hill towns in rock light, Giotto, Giorgione,
and later the edges of Cézanne's L'Estaque,

not for these things alone, and yet only
for what they were, themselves, my joy comes back.

2

From my father's cabinet I trace his predecessors
in a small blue book: *The English Topographical Draughtsmen,*

his pencil studies, delicately firm as theirs,
the lyrical, light precision of these craftsmen—

Girtin, Sandby, and Cotman, Peter De Wint,
meadows with needle spires in monochrome,

locks and canals with enormous clouds that went
rolling over England, postcards from home,

his namesake's county, Warwickshire. His own
work was a double portrait, a cherished oval

of his wife in oil, his own face, with a soft frown
that seemed to clarify the gentle evil

of an early death. A fine sketch of a cow,
a copy of Millet's *The Gleaners,* Turner's

The Fighting Téméraire, the gathering blow
of a storm with tossing gulls, more than a learner's

skill in them, more than mimicry, a gift.
But a ticking clerk in a colonial government,

his time stopped at the wharf where seagulls lift
and pick at a liner's wake in argument.

There nodding schooners confirmed their names
in oily water, in their Sabbath mooring,

but just as real were etchings of the Thames
by Whistler, coal docks and gulls soaring.

Cross-hatching strokes, and Battersea dividing,
and joining by division, the smoky Thames,

the same bronze stallion, its ringleted king riding,
the barges sliding where the broken water flames.

3

Without ever knowing my father it seems to me now
(I thought I saw him pause in the parenthesis

of our stairs once), from the blank unfurrowed brow
of his self-portrait, that he embodied the tenderness

of water, his preferred medium, its English reticence
but also its fragile delight, like a prediction

of his own passing, its tinted mist and essence,
and the verse that made him my precocious fiction.

The precise furrows of a landscape from which a lark arrows
while, under her parted hood, a blind girl listens,

some sunlit shire behind her, all with a rainbow's
benediction, the light that brims and glistens

like tears in Millais's work were like my mother's
belief in triumph over affliction. A peasant sows

his seeds with a scything motion, the lark's good news
is beyond his hearing, striding these humped furrows

a clod trampling clods in sabots, his wooden shoes
riding the troughs of ploughed soil, these boots

my father drew from Millet. These distant landscapes
which his devotion copied, did they despise the roots

and roofs of his island as inferior shapes
in the ministry of apprenticeship? Learning

did not betray his race if he copied a warship's
final berth, a cinder in a Turner sunset burning,

any more than the clouds that hid the lark's *trill-trill*,
or whatever its sound, behind creamy cumuli

over Pontoise, over the flecked Morne or grey hill
above Pontoise, or the stroke in a hound's thigh,

the stroke, the syllable, planted in the furrows
of page and canvas, in varnished pews whose doors

let in the surf of trees, carrying the echoes
of another light, of Venice, of Pontoise.

4

How little we had to go by! At the library window,
I remember one picture, *A Silvery Day near the Needles,*

bright wind on water, one I wanted to do
for its salt, fast clouds, sharp rocks were "the Needles."

Fragile little booklets, reproductions in monochrome,
RENOIR, DÜRER, several Renaissance masters

were our mobile museum, the back yards of home
were the squares of Italy, its piazzas our thick pastures.

Burnt hills that plunged the pilgrim into Umbria,
Giotto's grottoes, cliffs dotted with trees,

cities like colours, Siena; we could see the
Madonna's blue mantle in the sea around Canaries.

All that was radiant, complete, and lovely
was shared in secular ecstasy between us,

the apostolic succession of the
reproductions; Botticelli's Venus,

the stone arches winged like the kneeling
angel in Fra Angelico's *Annunciation*,

astonishing mastery, details revealing
themselves to rapturous examination.

A hill town in Mantegna, afternoon light
across Les Cayes, and dusks of golden wheat,

as pupils we needed both worlds for the sight:
of Troumassee's shallows at the Baptist's feet.

Paintings so far from life fermenting around us!
The skeletal, scabrous mongrels foraging garbage,

the moss-choked canals, back yards with contending odours
purifying in smoke, then to turn a sepia page

from the canals of Guardi, from a formal battle with banners,
the carnival lances of Uccello's pawing horses,

to the chivalric panoply of tossing green bananas
and the prongs of the ginger lily. No metamorphosis

was required by the faiths that made all one:
rock quarries with lions and crouched saints,

or raindrop and dewdrop in measured incantation
on the palm of a yam leaf, the communion of paints.

Whenever a conflagration of sea-almonds
and fat-pork bushes caught the brittle drought

and their copper leaves clattered over the Morne's
redoubts or Vigie barracks, my joy would shout

to the stained air, my body's weight through it
lighter than a spinning leaf, my young head

chattering with birdsong, a bird-pecked fruit;
I saw how the dove's wings were eyed and spotted

and how brief its flight was, but not how long
I would keep such lightness until my sins

crippled and caged me. I felt I would belong
to the dirt road forever, my palette's province,

an irrepressible April with its orange,
yellow, tan, rust, red, and vermilion note

on the bars of dry branches in a language
cooing one vowel from the shell of the dove's throat.

III

1

Flattered by any masterful representation
of things we knew, from Rubens's black faces

devoutly drawn, to the fountaining elation
of feathery palms in an engraving's stasis,

we caught in old prints their sadness, an acceptance
of vacancy in bent cotton figures

through monochrome markets, a distant tense
for a distant life, still, in some ways, ours.

The St. Thomas drawings have it, the taint
of complicit time, the torpor of ex-slaves

and benign planters, suffering made quaint
as a Danish harbour with its wooden waves.

And what of the world, burning outside the library,
the harbour's cobalt, every hot iron roof,

and its mongrel streets? That ordinary
alchemical indifference of youth

transformed by a page's altar, even then,
loved the false pastorals of Puvis de Chavannes,

until the light of redemption came with Gauguin,
our creole painter of *anses*, *mornes*, and *savannes*,

of olive hills, immortelles. He made us seek
what we knew and loved: the burnished skins

of pawpaws and women, a hill in Martinique.
Our martyr. Unique. He died for our sins.

He, Saint Paul, saw the colour of his Muse
as a glowing ingot, her breasts were bronze

under the palm of a breadfruit's fleur-de-lys,
his red road to Damascus through our mountains.

Saint Paul, Saint Vincent, in the hallowed toil
of crowning a wave, as green as our *savannes*

shining with wind; pouring linseed oil
and turpentine in cruses with scared hands.

Precious, expensive in its metal cruse,
and poured like secular, sacramental wine,

I still smell linseed oil in the wild views
of villages and the tang of turpentine.

This was the edge of manhood, this a boy's
precocious vow, sworn over the capped tubes

like a braced regiment, as his hand deploys
them to assault a barrack's arching cubes.

Where did we get the money from to paint?
Out in the roaring sun, each road was news,

and the cheap muscatel, bought by the pint?
Salt wind encouraged us, and the surf's white noise.

2

The turgid masonry of the village churches,
in scale provincial cathedrals, loomed over tin

fences and salt-bleached streets, their verges'
stagnant gutters. Rounding a mountain

road they held their station by a sea
of processional crests, saying their Rosaries

to the brown lace altars of Micoud and Dennery,
then, to leeward, softly, at Anse La Raye, Canaries,

Soufrière, Choiseul, Laborie, Vieux Fort, that were
given echoes drawn from the map of France,

its dukedoms pronounced in the verdant patois
of bamboo letters, a palm's sibilance.

There is a D'Ennery in the private maps
Pissarro did of his province, its apostrophe

poised like a gull over these furrowing whitecaps,
these distant breakers with their soundless spray.

Vernacular shallows muttered under bridges
on whose banks cane lances fluttered as the sail

of a wading egret rose towards the ridges
of mountain ferns until the roofs grew small.

The coastal road giddied down precipices
to the sweep of Dennery; two sea-gnawed islets

shielding its bay as they endured the size
of shawling Atlantic combers. Their sunsets

were rose as cathedral ceilings with saffron
canyons of cumuli. The chronology of clouds

contained the curled charts of navigation,
battles with smoke and pennants, shrouds

of settling canvas, as afternoon descended
past the cobalt wall of the sea to a faint

vermilion and orange, and the sky overhead
ripened to a Tiepolo ceiling. All was paint

and the light in paint, in the dusty olive
of Cézanne's trees, from Impressionist prints

the clumps of mangoes, from brush and palette knife,
Canaries framed in the cubes of Aix-en-Provence.

Fond St. Jacques, D'elles Soeurs, La Fargue, Moule à Chique
trees from Courbet and Corot, Bal en Bouche,

our landscapes emerging in French though we speak
English as we work. My pen replaced a brush.

3

I matched the first paragraph of *The Red and the Black*
in translation to a promontory on the sky of the page

resting on the harbour line with the recumbent arc
of the Vigie peninsula, across the sea from the college.

Even in translation a crispness in the Stendhal
shone from the barrack's gamboge arches, a prose

bracing in its width; so every village cathedral,
with its rusted zinc roofs through clumps of almonds, rose

in inheritance from Stendhal or Cézanne's L'Estaque,
the impasto indigo bay, the ochre walls of Provence,

organic examples from a verandah, the barrack
arches were Stendhal's brick consonants.

I resolved, from example, that nothing matched the vow,
not even a line of verse like a street with shacks,

a blue sea at the end of the line, that could show
the texture of grass in light, its little shocks.

4

Despite their middens' excremental stench,
their pristine rivulets so clogged with garbage,

the villages clung to a false pride, their French
namesakes, in faith, in carpentry, in language,

so that the harbour with its flour-bag sails,
the rusted vermilion of the market's roofs

made every wharf a miniature Marseilles
when, slow as a cloud, a high cruise ship arrives.

We saw it through guarded gates that shrank our stature,
it loomed as close as paradise and as forbidden;

it was a separate city, with its own legislature
of perfection, its braided ruler hidden.

Its immaculate officers lined up at the rails,
like settling gulls; then, with a long moan at dusk,

its cabin lights budded high over the lateen sails
of tree canoes, it blocked the sun's orange disc

and left us to empty streets and the lapping wharves
and the remembering bollards where it had moored,

to the astonished gossip of small waves,
and the light of cities in the word "abroad."

(**IV**)

1

I imagine him sketching the port, becoming a painter,
as the trade wind polishes Charlotte Amalie,

until the salt taste of the wind grows fainter
than the voices of his Sephardic family.

Sundays meant heat and songs from their sepulchral
piano, mahogany aunts stiff with palmetto fans,

doilies and dessert and, marshalled on the mantel,
the postcard cousins of a fading France.

Through jalousies that let the drifting sun
wander the stifling furniture, then rest

on the Armenian carpet, the afternoon
stays too long after lunch, a tiresome guest.

His gaze travels the shelves who now, by rote,
recite their stories from shell-bordered frames,

the wretched passage on the immigrant boat,
their soft eyes warm him. They whisper dates and names.

They quietly catalogue their origins:
the beards in oval light, next to them are

their spouses' paler ovals, hidden pins
holding their hair high, colonial haut bourgeois.

"In 1799 in the coastal city
of Bordeaux, in France, I, Joseph Pissarro,

your grandpère, was born. Anne Felicité Petit,
a Parisian, became my wife. Later, we go

with children and her brother, Isaac Petit,
to settle in St. Thomas. At first, the change

of light, the glare, the slaves, the burning sea
after a city built from fog seemed strange,

but then our children come and business
is good, so listen, my son Joseph's son,

this place is good, away from the world's noise,
but the old world must never be forgotten.

These Uncle Isaac married, each in turn,
two sisters from the island of Dominica;

there is a lesson in there you should learn,
the spirit is weak, but the flesh is weaker.

Esther and Rachel Manzano-Pomié,
your rigid great-aunts with their moles and noses

who secateured anything that crossed their way;
rebellious weeds, aristocratic roses,

as we took root in this well-modelled town,
our longing for that fogbound port grew fainter;

we pray that you (and here the portraits frown)
'follow the business, not turn into a painter.' "

2

A restlessness estranged him from each parent,
sullen and difficult, despite the beauty

of bays and flowering hills, a discontent
in ticking off lined ledgers, his family duty,

like going to synagogue. He only went
to keep up appearances, the ceremonial lie

darkened his doubt; doubt was the patron saint
for whom they named the island, the one

who had examined the sacred holes. Paint
meant deliverance from dawn's crucifixion.

He dreaded the nightmare of remaining forever
in his uncle's odorous shed, keeping ledgers straight;

its African torpor with spasms of endeavour;
the sea's blue door locked at the end of the street.

Here was a new world: in faith, in form, in feature,
in blaze and shadow, in tints beneath black skin:

the wet light moving down the ebony fissure
of a fisherman's shoulders as he hauled in a seine,

a black dog panting for entrails near a pirogue
on sand so white it blinded, a sea so blue

it stained your hand, not epilogue but prologue
a new world offered him, but his impatience grew.

3

He sketched the flecked bay of Charlotte Amalie
across which a swallow shot like a skimmed stone,

longer than his vow to leave work and family
and join that skein of smoke trawling the horizon.

Was this true, his shadow moving over the barrels
of codfish, is the hope of his exile betrayal?

How are his thoughts different from the local quarrels
of the waves at his shoes, isn't his the old trial

of love faced with necessity, the same crisis
every island artist, despite the wide benediction

of light, must face in these barren paradises
where after a while love becomes an affliction?

4

Despite mornings of continuous generosity
in inlets, on hills, on harbours with their quiet wharves,

and in feathery skies the cirrus's sweeping scarves,
did he stand on the still wharf and long for a city

with the smoke of stations, fog, the black strokes of crowds,
gables and mansards, a longing for the centre,

for the portals of gilt frames his gift could enter
like a museum door? Paris with its echoing words,

its delicate boulevards, carriages, tremulous greys,
names as old as its light, Raspail, Montparnasse,

not the brick alleys of Charlotte Amalie, the quays
and the quarrelsome wharves? I see their shadows pass

over barrels near the odorous schooners
that connect islands with their squawking freight.

He walks with his mentor, Melbye, through the noise
of the radiant market, planning their flight.

Stares probe him, their fishing needles sewing
nets in the broad-blade shadows of the teak,

their mouths stitched shut. "We know you going.
We is your roots. Without us you weak."

This by a canal clogged by chutes of coal
stewing in garbage, smells that rose in rain,

while fish scales in the market swayed his soul,
balancing both worlds. In which should he remain?

(V)

1

These feathery engravings have not altered much:
the madras roar of stalls, and inevitably,

some one-legged veteran hobbling on a crutch
with singing stump through Charlotte Amalie.

Passing them, his fingers frame every trade:
the wooden chips caught in the springy hair

of a carpenter's daughter from his whirring blade;
the cobbler's coffin-doorway, his repair

of soles in their shoe cemetery with his last,
the Egyptian smell of polish; the cabinetmaker

near the wreck where urchins leap into the past;
the meandering reek of rum that could wake the

nostrils of dead fishermen, rattling homemade
carts with the stink of gutted fish on the shorefront;

the settlement with its twisting lanes of mud
that followed the bare foot; all he could want.

Arches, with incongruous Africans, erected by the Danes
in an echo of Copenhagen, like his uncle's store.

The streets were troughs of mud after the rains,
the same hand that totalled bills learning to draw.

The full moon's dial ticked the monotony
of their grooved life: temple, store, and house,

their secular devotion to save money
as well as soul. The tedium of hot hours!

And the fierce glint of metallic afternoons
from fern verandahs! He had drawn enough

of these, though he'd enjoyed them once;
now they glared back with an expected love.

2

He studied a black mongrel's cowering lope,
how it stood, out of range, assessing its tormentor,

ribs panting, its eyes with no fleck of hope,
resigned to its limits, the doors it could not enter.

He watched clouds build on the grey side of the mountain,
its quartz road glittering in a spasm of sun,

then the bay brighten in panic, before rain
really rolled down the hills with the noise of a wagon.

The rain walked across the harbour, then, leisurely,
up to the warehouse door; it almost smothered

the sting of cod, of coffee sacks. The sea
disappeared, nails drummed the tin roof of the shed

and the gutters steamed. This was the other season,
the siege of slanting lances, flowering water,

the warehouse darkened, an odorous prison
where he was sentenced to the labourers' laughter.

The synonymous endurance of an insult
came with the umber and ebony of their skin,

from a sea wind that healed by adding its salt
to their wounds, from manacle, from festering chain,

even in the light of threshing palms, whose fronds
Melbye urged him to master, even in coarse cotton

frocks and straw hats, as they made their rounds
through the market, to the quick edge of town.

A gift already assembling itself for departure,
although light defined his delight in the wharves,

like a Dutch engraving. Falsify his rapture,
and more, falsify this plea from former slaves:

stunned, perhaps, by their sudden manumission,
they drifted like zombies from their sugar estate.

A clatter of pigeons mimicked their position,
their circling flight. Freedom was their new fate.

Monumental vendors offered their fruit trays
with the glare of Gorgons, and forgiving cripples

who knew his uncle, he ignored their cries.
He and Melbye floated through their silent appeals.

"Halt, one foot on the gangplank! Turn, become us,
master and patriarch, let bearded spray confirm it,

your birthright; be in obscure St. Thomas
our Giotto, our Jerome, our rock-hidden hermit!"

3

When the rainy season laid siege to the house,
bringing an Egyptian infestation of beetles,

BOY ON A WALL, RAT ISLAND, 1989
Watercolour on paper, 7½″ x 10″
Mrs. Judy Chastanet

multiplying the flies of August, spies for its powers,
the climate mimicking winter, without cold, in heatless

clouds with their sombre presumption of wisdom
over this superficial sunshine, the tiring bliss

of perpetual summer, every thunderhead's dome
was Sacré-Coeur, the grey wisdom of Paris.

He and Melbye in fact fled to Venezuela,
and remained there for years, till the day came

when the first step had to be taken, to tell the
story, familiar obscurity to unfamiliar fame.

What would have been his future had he stayed?
He was Art's subject as much as any empire's,

he had no more choice than the ship that steered
with its black chimneys and volcanic fires.

4

Those islands, seen one rung of judgement lower
than their own estimate from a steamship's ladder

despite cerulean bays with hills in flower,
and postcard streets, fine as Dronningens Gade,

and bursting markets and abandoned forts
and ruined windmills and postage-stamp parks

with arching teak or banyan are all ports
of sunshot vacancy: a brochure's remarks.

Perhaps he saw their emptiness in terror
of what provided nothing for his skill

until his very birthplace was an error
that only flight might change, and exile kill.

The Old World lay ahead, the New receding,
its primal Edens soon exhaust their use,

the Old is subtler, varied, with more breeding,
given its history what should he choose?

Shadows and shanties, shade-crossed bamboo paths,
its fragrant forests never penetrated,

and narrow falls with white, cascading baths,
and parrots screaming betrayal overhead

from saffron ceilings over Santa Cruz,
and flame trees fading into indigo

over brown, rumorous brooks? They had their use.
The new had gotten old. He had to go.

The day has come, the word widens: "Abroad."
The steamship is furrowing these heaving

troughs of the Atlantic, the deep reversing road
of the diaspora, Exodus, the last gull leaving.

France will translate him, he will find his voice
in its hoarse lindens, a boulevard's sentence,

couplets of silvery aspens whispering "Pontoise,"
its roads opening like an inheritance.

As the last headland hazed he turned to enjoy
the slow swells spuming from the Atlantic winds,

guy wires singing of that city he knew as a boy,
to the exultant treachery of dolphins.

BOOK TWO

1

Irascible rain threshed in the cedar leaves,
its roar a conch shell's voices in his ears;

blackbirds kept arguing in the fretwork eaves
that they were sparrows, and the sea noise: Paris.

He lay in bed and listened to the surf
below the greying window and a train's

moan, like the mail boat's, every Sabbath.
He rose and drew the lightly surging curtains.

Light. The island vanished. A grey light
reticent, on the roofs, the spires, the domes,

and the trees between them, on hills, the white
strokes of more walls, more spires, more domes,

and chimneys with their soundless exclamations
and the sea-loud avenue; nothing was black,

not even the shadow-chasms; width and patience
of various indigos. Her prodigal was back.

There was no fury in this light, no glare
of exultation like his island sky;

instead, its very pigment was the air,
as soft in exhalation as a sigh.

The light of France disgorges History
through a stone dolphin. The leaf-soft squares

of his schooling still speak French. The sky
repeats great canvases, dazedly he wanders

the incredible topiary of Versailles,
down its infinite avenues, each sadder

and unconsoling to his salting eyes
than the bright breezes of Dronningens Gade.

Dronningens Street. Cobbles under soles. Packed
tight as a mosaic. Drying from drizzle. Glistening.

Shoes scuffling to the melody of fact
that is history. Horned tritons listening.

The sculptor's chisel makes his nereids antic
in their frilled basin, in light gusts of spray

priapic dolphins arch from the Atlantic,
their gurgling spigots fill his memory.

Memory that strains to recognise which Quarter,
its map of veins? He's lost. Where's this place? In

awe of the mesmeric lure of water,
the nereids in their tinkling, shell-lipped basin,

he hears the same noise in the chuckling bilge
of anchored schooners. No, no, not the same!

This metropolitan mutter spelt privilege,
each noun in Paris echoed with its fame.

Museums demean him. Island boy. The eye
of a crazed duke pursues him up the stairs

of the Louvre to halt at this couplet as I
did for the grazing hound. At night, he hears

ENGLISH GARDEN, STRATFORD-ON-AVON, 1991
Watercolour on paper, 10″ x 14″
Dr. & Mrs. Christopher Beaubrun

a litany of great names, Goya, Velázquez,
but marbles turn their heads away from him,

from ancient texts in his Sephardic eyes,
glances in which the Seine's swift swallows skim;

and, as he drifts and mutters, aimlessly,
jealousy pierces him, until he freezes

before the gold heat of a Tiepolo sky,
down tiring colonnades of masterpieces.

None, none are his! Gold helmets, cuirasses,
hard, burnished halberds in the wrinkling murk

of vanished forests whose warriors were as
dead as the huge frames that embalmed their work;

nor the musculature in thigh and tendon
of naked deities barely treading grass,

nor goddesses borne upward, backward bending
on Mars' elbow, his sun-defying brass.

A Franz Hals head borne on its dish of lace,
the Venice of Guardi in its wriggling mesh

of poling gondolas, Rembrandt's self-portraits
in gnawing darkness as light leaves his flesh.

His stomach aches. Drained, he waits
on a bench for confidence to return

as dusk ignites the Louvre and the gates
of immense clouds close. Trees burn

to ash, but he is their citizen. His
the bracing, incandescent cafés,

the rhyme of his stroll repeating Paris, Paris,
the pallor of daybreak on a frightened canvas.

Such fears, such exaltations! Even the rain
gusting across her lamps had history,

strong as her fiction the grey confirming Seine
flowed with a force that hallowed memory.

With every breaking sunrise his joy builds,
but with it an anxiety in his ardour

for France's brightening roofs, her halls and guilds,
for Notre Dame, the weight of history's shadow.

2

And the pitch nights over her streets were starry
as the pavements with their banks of yellow flowers

whose names he never knew, or that would vary
from their names in the islands, and showers

fell against window light and streetlamp
and glazed the boulevards to a blurred prism

streaked like a window glass or when the damp
paper wriggled with Impressionism.

Perhaps he stared into a brazier's embers
and saw the flame trees on ridges of blue smoke

when autumn's flare cindered to grey November's,
the island's sun still in him when he woke.

His name, Pissarro, hidden in the word Paris,
and, twigs on the tremulous Seine, the sound: Camille.

More than Dronningens Gade, they are his,
as, once, the slow flailing of a sugar mill.

In a sugar-factory yard labourers gather
to the smell of wet earth and newly greased

machines in the breathing sunrise, as their
ochre pot hounds forage, not at the Feast

of Levi, but for scraps of garbage. None
has the arched white grace of a whippet

or wolfhound. The yard, in the widening sun,
has a pool of molasses. Ochre dogs sip it.

There are no Negroes in the pantheon
of bleached albino marbles that were painted

with the garish taste of an Asiatic sun,
but in generous frescoes he grows acquainted

with hounds and turbanned Moors at the edge of a feast.
Make your own masterpieces, don't copy ours,

nor join in an arc the wolfhound and this beast
in a hovel's shade, outside brass-studded doors.

St. Thomas meant the clouding of ambition,
its lowered sail a shirt draped on a chair,

its sorrow, the paint stains crusting an apron,
its past the weight of dust on furniture.

His alley echoes to a sculptor's mallet,
stone chips on floors, grey light on grey glass,

the changing complexion of his palette.
Rustling addresses: Raspail, Montparnasse.

3

A lengthening sorrow, a sinuous sigh of smoke
wandered over Paris's autumnal freight yards,

it rose with his homesickness when he woke,
it hovered over charred chimneys and carved mansards

all day in an iron sky. He had made his choice:
the crowded stations, the dark arriving quickly,

the sun at the fog's core, the ordered chaos
from which the smoke escaped, his silent cry.

Out walking he turned a corner with the same
view through screening trees and the dome

of an unnamed chapel, a familiar frame.
And then a black dog crossed it. He was home.

The days were a grey drizzle, the same days
over and over; their subtleties would emerge

from repetition, through the elegiac haze
drawing its widow's veil across a church.

Umbrellas blossomed from the avenues' furrows
with mist and steam in autumn's irrigation,

mixed with the smell of horse dung, flowers
blazed on the pavement of St. Lazare station.

In the island, besieged by paralysing rain,
all motion stopped, people stood in arches

brooding on the sluices from the clouded mountain,
the flooding gutters mounting by quick inches

while mongrels miserably shook their dank fur
in a spray of diamonds, and sloped towards the dark

holes under the shacks; the light grew heavier
and the island dipped like an untethered ark.

4

There is nothing to see except the rain
on beaded Paris, through soiled window glass,

the water seeds in furrows, grain by grain,
shrouding Raspail, erasing Montparnasse,

but from all this, from edges indistinct
as mass, through the dissolving drizzle,

crowds, carriages, and linden lamps are linked
by the rain's brushstrokes, with fresher skill.

Doubt was his patron saint, it was his island's,
the saint who probed the holes in his Saviour's hands

(despite the parenthetical rainbow of providence)
and questioned resurrection; its seven bright bands.

Saint Thomas, the skeptic, Saint Lucia, the blind
martyr who on a tray carried her own eyes,

the hymn of black smoke, wreath of the trade wind,
confirming their ascent to paradise.

Boucher and Fragonard were the accepted masters
(bedchamber dramas with rhapsodical faintings),

battles, or golden cattle in luminous pastures,
and the Barbizon school. As for his paintings

he did not so much finish as surrender them
as hostages to hope. Doubt made him yield,

his brush a sword reversed; when dusk came,
he set down his bleeding palette like a shield.

Silence woke him. He lay still. It had quieted
and muffled the roar of the street. He knew

that it probably was the blizzard everyone said
was coming, furring the railings of the avenue.

He rose. The sky was shedding flakes like a bolster
feathering the city of his childhood, the wonder

of forgotten snow. He felt his lost soul stir
as innocence whitened and crusted the window

to a primed surface. Snow inched up the sill
with remarkable thickness and speed, until

Paris was a blank canvas. Its cloud was still.
He dressed, rushed out, and walked through the miracle.

(VII)

1

Falling from chimneys, an exhausted arrow—
he watched a swallow settling on its ledge;

its wings wrote "Paris" from the name "Pissarro,"
a brush lettering a cloud's canvas edge.

The studio was cavernously cold. In their
jars, bristles froze, but he was determined,

when spectres snubbed him in the ashen air,
to erase his island as the knifing wind

sharpened its blade on lampposts, that homecoming
glowed from the orange windows of his street,

groping up steps to feel his body humming
like the stove's belly with malarial heat.

Needles of icy rain, swivelling slush,
head down against their onslaught were still his

more than the snowdrops on an evergreen bush,
those lamps in daylight, the stiff smoke of chimneys.

Wasn't the old persecution still possession?
His history emerged in the half-light

of Rembrandt's gaze, and Saskia's thighs that shone,
brightening a pool, his heritage by right.

Silk hats, their asphalt sheen, hazed Notre Dame,
wet, wriggling reflections, chestnuts in braziers,

horse dung and drizzle, all were his to claim
by drawing on the fog's careful erasures.

A brushstroke flicks a whip, and a carriage lurches
from the leaf-shade of lindens, a grey stallion

clops down lime avenues, past famous churches
joining hyphens in a sprinkling carillon,

a page of the boulevard opens, smoke, cirrus above
Baudelaire's *"fourmillante cité,"* a bursting anthill

of crowds and carriages, quick strokes make them move,
in time with bell and whip, stanza and canticle.

The lark of an acolyte's voice climbs from the choir
from a city that worships Sundays, parks, and prams,

and the clouds of a Tiepolo ceiling, their saffron fire,
a sky that it shares with his island's rusted palms.

2

O, the exclamation of white roses, of a wet
grey day of glazed pavements, the towers

in haze of Notre Dame's silhouette
in the Easter drizzle, lines banked with flowers

and umbrellas flowering, then bobbing like mushrooms
in the soup-steaming fog! Paris looked edible:

salads of parks, a bouillabaisse of fumes
from its steaming trees in the incredible

fragrance of April; and all this would pass
into mist, even cherishable mud, the delicate

entrance of tentative leaves and the grass
renewed when the sun opened its gate.

The Renaissance, brightening, had painted altars,
ceilings, cupolas, feasts with an arched dog,

this city's painters, the guild in her ateliers
made her sublime and secular as fog.

3

Since light was simply particles in air,
and shadow shared the spectrum, strokes of paint

are phrases that haphazardly cohere
around a point to build an argument,

vision was not the concentrated gaze
that took in every detail at a glance.

Time, petrified in every classic canvas,
denied the frailty of the painter's hands,

acquired an intimacy with its origin, Claude,
David, and the Venetian schools presumed

a privilege given by the gods or God,
while Time's blasphemous fire consumed, consumed.

Now sunlight is splintered and even shade is entered
as part of the prism, and except for its defiant

use in Manet, black is a coiled tube drying
from neglect, the classical drama of painting is interred

with Courbet's *The Funeral*. Landscape as theatre,
shadow as melodrama without damnation,

buried with the painter's belief in a Creator
who balanced evil and light in one dimension,

shade lost its moral contrast, doubt disappears
in the moment's exaltations, in flowers and loaves

as a loaf in Chardin belittles the girls in Greuze
with its solid denial, the death behind his still lifes.

In those still lifes, where dying rings like crystal
from glasses polished by a servant's breath,

lay the sweet pain of the Impressionists. All
natures-morts are altars laid for Death.

The metallic shine of a gaping mackerel,
the ring in its dead eye like a Vermeer earring;

that highlight on its skin sharpening smell.
There mastery lay in Manet, the same daring

that caught the vermilion light in a hound's thigh,
one stroke on the dog and the staring mackerel,

the spectral animal at *The Feast of Levi*,
licking her outstretched hand, shared the one skill.

But what conviction was carried in a sketch,
and patchy impasto surfaces with dim drawing?

What authority granted the privilege
of blurring, dissolving, ignoring form, outlawing

detail of trees without Corot's feathery grace?
Physics had analysed light into particles floating

and the Pointillist muse was Science; all space
was a concentration of dots, picnickers boating

on the summer Seine, dogs, parasols. Their refusers
rejected this change of vision, of deities; theories

instead of faith, geometry, not God. Their accusers
saw them as shallow heretics, unorthodox painters

using wriggles for tree trunks, charred twigs for figures,
crooked horizons, shadows streaked with purple;

they were the Academy's outcasts, its niggers
from barbarous colonies, a contentious people!

They followed impulse, with no concern for their craft,
geese that lacked the concentration of swans,

their brushstrokes wriggling necks. The Salon laughed
as it locked them out. Sketches. Impressions.

They were heretical in their delight,
there was no deity outdoors, no altar,

in the rose window of the iris, light
was their faith, a shaft in an atelier.

4

The Refused, the Rejected, they collected there:
Café Guerbois, close to la Place de Clichy,

indulging this anarchist, arms flailing the air,
who would burn the Louvre, Bazille, Monet, Sisley.

Bazille, who had the shyness of a ladder,
whose height of voice was often paralysing.

Sisley, who was sad and who kept getting sadder,
and sour Degas; all had this gift of satirising

the Salon. But they were still citizens,
Frenchmen, for all their mockery of the centre,

who staked their plots: Givenchy or Provence;
who shared an intimacy he could not enter,

keeping his distance like that homeless dog
that followed them on Sundays on the wharf

past the dry palms of their modest synagogue,
white walls and bougainvilleas; yet none

contained the oracular secret of his name
that enclosed their city as his very own.

Writing in *Le Temps*, the critic Paul Mantz
reassured the public about these Impressionists:

"There is no need to fear that ignorance
will ever become a virtue," so the public resists.

A painting by Renoir fetches 47 francs,
a public auction bleeds its crippling lists.

His own were 50 francs. "They have heavy hands,"
said *Le Temps*. Brushes in brute fists.

The *shul* forbade any representation
of graven images, but Art is secular;

he wore his heresy with resignation
an acolyte shedding his scapular.

Besides, in Pontoise there were farms and churches
in secular sunlight, they would be his Madonnas,

candle-shaped, a white cart that lurches
under angelic rooks, their hoarse hosannas.

VIII

1

The surge of summer lifted the park trees
like breakers cresting, waiters flapped the sails

of tablecloths and billowed them. The Tuileries
blossomed with children, black iron sills

and balconies, and fierce cobalt skies,
the cries of gulls and nurses, their white cries

recalled those Sundays of Charlotte Amalie's
and the bays of his childhood's paradise.

In a straw chair, by the Seine's blue tablecloth,
its sails like peaked napkins, the white-walled Aegean,

he is pierced by the lances of Charlotte Amalie's wharf,
gulls' handkerchiefs fluttering against the green.

The boulevards turn Mediterranean
with puff clouds, awnings, flowers on balconies,

straw hats and sailboats, and along the Seine
an oceanic surging in the trees.

All day the sky reset its linen tables,
smoothed them and scraped their crumbs. His lifted

heart darted like a sparrow between gables
and mansards, pecking at its daily bread.

He felt as grateful as the trembling bird
for his survival, cautious of each chance,

febrile, alert if the least gesture stirred,
then practising the strategy of patience.

He kept a routine strict as a metronome;
after work, the bright café. They saved his chair.

A cognac, crumbs of gossip, then home
for a precise, modest supper. Eating, he would hear

the dark voice of Rachel singing her Moroccan
lament as grating as the blowing dunes

of her lost desert, Oh, go back again
to your dry date palms and whirling Bedouins!

But on the stairs once, paused on the landing
(as I did for the hound), he heard her soft

sobbing for her language and, not understanding
why he should share her tears, climbed to his loft.

The sun fled south. Damp soaking to his soul.
The island blazed at the back of his mind

like the black stove, a dilating coal
before it turned emerald in the evening wind.

2

Black downpours on a clouded, dripping day,
tinkle of rain like cutlery in the leaves,

pencil-thin drizzle. Deep in the brown café
he watched ropes of water twisting from the eaves.

This was the hangout: the Café Guerbois,
a nest of anarchists, syndicalists,

a roar of theories from the artistic bores
and bums whose principle was getting pissed.

The waitress at his sawdust café liked this gentle guy,
his gaze direct and round as the Postman Roulin's,

his conversations discreet, but a mischievous eye
measured her parenthetical hips, her ample lines.

"In Paris everyone is a painter." She shrugged a shoulder
to prove it. She should visit his atelier;

he was born in paradise, a far island, and the older
he got, the more he missed it. His work was a failure,

but he didn't mind. She came at the end of the day.
Did she like his paintings? Yes. When would they be finished?

The new way they painted now looked hurried anyway
compared to the past. The autumn dusk diminished

in a lilac sky, the petals of lamps came on
while she sat by the window sipping tea he brought her,

lifting and placing the porcelain teacup down
with a geisha's precision, with tinkling laughter.

He reached for her hand and she simply surrendered
a bare palm to his. He kissed its mound. She withdrew it

and rose to go, but there was life, not dread
in the shaft of that grace, and she knew that he knew it.

His life was a steamship in the harbour, turning,
the vanes of a sugar mill reversing their steady flail

once the meridian was crossed. There was no returning
like the African wind that kept billowing the canvas's sail.

3

He looked from the window for her until she crossed
to the pavement opposite, where she turned, then kissed

her palm (the same one), and waved it. Then her hat tossed
on the crowd's current. He wiped the brush in his fist.

The kiss darted like a swallow through the dusk, slipping
past darkening gables to join the settling fleet

of its companions; he heard the pigeons gossiping
from the eaves that he'd frightened her into flight.

But he knew they both carried the shaft of benediction
of that half-hour, even if, like a leaf in a canal, she swirled

into her own life, another part of Paris. I painted this fiction
from the hound's arch, because over the strokes and words

of a page, or a primed canvas, there is always the shadow
that stretches its neck like a spectral hound, bending

its curious examining arc over what we do,
both at our work's beginning and at its ending,

a medieval *memento mori*, or a boy with his arrow
at a dog-eared page or blank canvas, for every artisan

a skull and a pierced heart. This was true of him now, Pissarro,
as it was in the still lifes of his friend Cézanne.

4

In that epiphanic moment that passed between them,
welding them in the warmth of commingling palms,

HEADLAND IN DROUGHT, 1997
Oil on canvas, 24″ x 30″

there was fear of the passing world. No one had seen them,
but one day he tired of the torment of her busy arms

and changed cafés. Years later, when he moved to a house,
she soared from his poplars, she was the inaudible lark

lost in a canvas cloud. A swallow carried her voice
across Paris's saffron sky as its roofs grew dark.

Excitement could burst his heart. This landscape was
to be looked at tearfully, with not a schoolboy's eyes

but a prodigal son's. The loss of St. Thomas
shone in the hermitage of his new home: *Pontoise*.

IX

1

Pont-oise: in effect, the bridge over the river
Oise, a tight village close to Paris. The Oise,

a branch of the coiling Seine, was soon the giver
of roots and swaying shade on the stone of his house.

Daybreak flings wide the windows of his eyes.
What waits beyond their beading frames should be

Adam unlatching the gate of Paradise,
but he walks through an insubstantial sea,

the fog that had forgotten him, as fog forgets,
which is its nature, to erase Nature

from the slow, spectral meadows it first wets
with drizzle to make extinction sure,

like a soaked aquarelle where oaks have frayed
their edges into cloud and rushes spout

under a wavering spire that will fade
into an outline to deepen the fog's doubt.

Foghorns from the slow barges on the Oise
sounded like cattle bellowing from the ropes

of mist that moored them, a desolating noise,
like boulders moaning on the scudding slopes.

The Barbizon school was entering its eclipse
even with Daubigny and the feathery glades

of Corot, whose altar was a votive wisp
of woodsmoke, its olive and umber shades.

An age, the size of a cloud over a wood,
erased all myth; slow intellectual doubt

diminished awe. In groves whose oaks once showed
a pillared piety, faith was going out

of their leaves, and a damp darkness absorbed
their trunks, their paths and pierced byways

haunted no more by ogres, a pale bed
of mould where a silvine reverence was.

By now the hallowed pastorals were besieged
by factories, stations, by the charred verticals

of factories' chimneys, palm stumps on a beach
that made the imperilled poplars precious, the calls

of dove and skylark rarer, till every
frame held bending smoke and the raw noise

of industry. He painted the ordinary
for what it was, not eulogies of Pontoise.

With all the excitement of an immigrant
prodigal with confirmations, he finds scenes

with echoing frames that are now his to paint:
red rutted roads, the lanes of Louveciennes.

He paints in dialect, like an islander,
in a fresh France; when his swayed poplars tilt

you catch an accent in their leaves, or under
his formal clouds a hill's melodic lilt.

A prism of broken glass flashed at the roots
of an oracular oak seized by the light,

it lit the shadows and the radial shoots
of his iris. It charted his new palette.

The poplars on ridges were the strokes of chimneys,
hedges shaped like trains, the spears of cypresses

as fixed as railings. A sky that was Veronese's
silkened its country evenings; but home distresses.

The heartbeat of every culture is its markets,
he remembered the straw-hatted vendors and the mounds

of earth-crusted vegetables, and his palette's
explosion of primal colours, the African sounds

of their shouts and bargains in Charlotte Amalie,
compared to the wet grey smells of cavernous sheds

in Paris, the reek of fish, the butcher's alley
with its gaping carcases, their virulent reds;

then the market women swaying down red roads
with blazing fruit, their baskets' colours,

mangoes, orange pawpaws, shifting their loads
in step with the drumming windmills of Pontoise.

2

A wall. Shadow-splashed, a limestone alley
with its leaping pattern of leaf-light and shade,

did Louveciennes reprint Charlotte Amalie,
its lanes those Sundays down Dronningens Gade?

It sank in him, like an interior stain,
an ineradicable blotch on plaster

at whose base moss and its slow stench remain
a flaw that neither skill nor prayer could master,

views whose nobility turned mediocre
from his mechanical blotches, and whose

range grew simple, olive, umber, ochre,
his outlines smothered in a hundred hues

to falsify delight, that brought his sadness
to roads with light-touched ruts and orange roofs

and a despair whose stain edged towards madness
and Time whose clock was a cart horse's hooves

under huge clouds not blinding white but tinted
from the ground below, earth colours at their base.

Time casts the hurtling shadows that are printed
on the Pontoise road, the bridge, the shallows' lace

between talkative aspens and small muttering roofs,
brown, purple, orange, each no more than a dab.

Time works on a rough cart's inaudible hooves
and a burst of rooks from a hayrick. A figure in a cap

gathers wood near a tree trunk, an invisible brook
is linked to the tinkling Oise past terraces

of tilled earth, he has learnt to look
at the instant with no pretext of stasis.

Submission to the Academy. Again. Again rejection.
A predictable plot, but still painful, the atelier

window to launch the act of dejection—
comic despair, that flailing leap of failure!

3

He and his friend Cézanne worked side by side
on a view of Louveciennes. They signed it together

in indistinguishable friendship. But deep inside,
Cézanne had moved further away, a change of weather

without a change of heart. Whatever they shared
was invaluable, incalculable; in the end

they were different, the pupil now dared
more than the master, without losing a friend.

Cézanne stayed close to two years in Pontoise,
attentive to his older friend's advice

to change his dingy palette to colours
brightened by his tutor's tropical eyes,

a different language for a different light,
more crystalline, more broken like the sea

on island afternoons, scorchingly bright
and built in prisms. He should learn to see.

But the pupil proceeded hesitantly
by daubs and gouts of cautious brilliance,

his brush ankling the depths then, arrogantly:
the monumental master of Provence.

The practice of modulation by a succession
of square, progressive strokes transformed a canvas

THE CHESS PLAYER, 1994
Watercolour on paper, 22½″ x 30″

by Cézanne to a musical score. This was not Impression
but visible syntax; a plaster cupidon, a blue vase

balanced on a tilted table, a canted horizon
and the planes of perspective challenge reason,

an idiosyncratic symmetry, a private grammar
and brutal geometry. Paint had, until then,

pretended it wasn't paint, but now an equal drama
was made of every inch, the artist as artisan,

as mason and plasterer, or notes from an instrument
defying a melody like words in Stein,

now stroke or word or note presume their intent
because of what they are: shape, sound, and stain,

compelled to one direction, an edge, a margin,
a page, a frame, a phrase of melody, where error

was part of the acceptance of their origin,
narrative held up to a left-handed mirror

that became an orthodoxy, though our inheritance
as acolytes was in the printed masterpieces

of museum missals, coloured pages of Cézanne's
gross ecstasies, his massive awkward figures, these

in Phaidon's series opened the gates of an empire
to applicants from its provinces and islands,

in the old argument that the great works we admire
civilise and colonise us, they chain our hands

invisibly. Museums seen as magnetic prisons
for the gifted exile, the self-diminishing ceiling

of a baroque glory more humbling than the sun's
predictable blue, till the exile sits, reeling

with astonishment, in the tints of Tiepolo's sky,
in the yellowing linen of a still life by Chardin,

in that stroke of light that catches a hound's thigh,
the paint is all that counts, no guilt, no pardon,

no history, but the sense of narrative time
annihilated in the devotion of the acolyte,

as undeniable as instinct, the brushstroke's rhyme
and page and canvas know one empire only: light.

Light on the wharves of Charlotte Amalie,
light on the sparkling straits of Sicily,

or where the exact light down a brick alley
translates de Hooch into a brilliant lie.

4

Over every Dutch interior there hovers
the hallucination of a narrative, so his background believes

in the intimacies of landscape, in light that covers
a kitchen wall, a milk jug with its crusted loaves,

as it does a countryside, so that even his boulevards
are the first lines of some fiction, a canvas will open

like a window in Zola, brushstrokes instead of words,
both fictions sharing a single eye, that of a pen.

Air! Air and light! A privacy externalised,
an open page crossed by the letters of leaves;

the light of islands, its magnitude realised
in a spring sky; that cloud where the lark lives.

(X)

1

Yet, in contrast to the lark's ecstatic soaring,
his luck sank lower; swirling with dejection,

like a kitchen sink. His canvases were boring.
He endorsed the Salon's by his own rejection.

Children and debts, a wife unshakeably morose,
his hair, early snow, thinning foam. He envied

the oak's fortitude, enduring the whistling blows
of storms. He laboured, but could not provide.

Debt caused quarrels. With Melbye. Corot. His own
brushwork turned frantic, angrier, weeds grew

in these furrows, their unstable horizon—
what was he but a backward, colonised Jew?

The blow of their rejection was a dull
ache that sat like an anvil on his heart,

all he had made in joy, thought beautiful,
in their directness was indifferent art,

the pavement pictures of an islander
struggling with every stroke to realise

a life not his, work whose earnest candour
retained a primal charm to expert eyes.

There is a kind of ecstasy to failure,
just as, at the heart of desire, is a core

of sweetness, the worm that whispered its lure
in white orchards. Crows with their critical caw.

The studio, with its stillness of failure,
was like a parlour where there had been a death;

shrouds of despair covered the atelier;
each canvas stared back, drew its last breath

and expired. They died on him, one by one,
they repeated their dying when he tried to find

the way that a desolate day seeks a streak of sun
on a strip of pavement, a spire, a window blind.

Success at home meant nothing, this was the centre
of opinion; for a Danish colonial Jew

from a dirty, backward island to enter
the museum's bronzed doors, that would never do.

So he tempted his pride with that tribal excuse
of his primitive Sephardic roots, but then, all the others

in the Salon des Refusés, weren't they also Jews?
And a landscape could not reject him with silence.

The seasonal hypocrisy of his surfaces
barely concealed his panic, trembling concern,

the repetition of barely varied places,
redone, knowing the pittance they might earn,

increased compulsion to a slow treadmill
of canvases, each view lightly altered,

street corner, kitchen garden, terraced hill;
but fear forced strength. His output never faltered.

While the melody of money is repeated
with every stroke, with every signature,

a tune he cannot shake from his head,
that sings like gnats around the drying picture,

the delight in light remains unaffected,
till even his greys have joy, his indigo,

all of that muted bliss contained in a red
rusting roof, an ochre wall, patches of snow.

2

By forty, bald, he looks twice that old, as
from his alpine dome, a beard's avalanche

cascades between the banks of sloping shoulders,
silvered with ash as a brown autumn branch,

but at that age, unchanged, he did not want
to be any different than when he would write

in his uncle's ledgers, still an accountant,
since painting is the chronicle of light,

content to be the weather's actuary,
the season's clerk, the eremite who drew

its Book of Hours, to whom its ordinary
hills and leaf-hachured lanes were always new.

Neige. Auberge. His strokes rhyme couplets now,
like the twin paintings of a brown inn in snow,

with horses waiting, and blurred trees below
the dim sky's cataract. His eyes begin to go,

BAITING THE HOOK, *c.* 1984
Oil on canvas, 36" x 30"

but his wrist flies, as accurate as a crow,
towards the skeletal branches, with its caw

scraping the frozen sky, his brushes know
the clouds as well as rooks, and perhaps more.

They organised an auction for him and Sisley,
but very little, even of that, came in the end.

He fretted in despair. He gave in too easily.
He should learn from the pliant poplars how to bend.

His wife, Julie, stumbled among the harvesters
to help keep the house. Their debts were growing

higher than summer grass. His investors
were the canvases, but too much was owing.

Her hands grew harder than his. Their veins rose
like vines. Cheekbones like scythes. Hollows

circled her eyes like crows. Beyond the house
she grew reed-thin, muttering like the Oise.

She was crazed with debt. He hoped they would forgive her,
for whatever she did, she needed rest;

she thought of carrying the two children to the river
and drowning them with her, she was that depressed.

But none of this meant anything to their father
whose arrogance did nothing to accommodate

her desperation, which meant he would rather
they perished than pawn his work. Whose word was "Wait."

In gales of depression, at the house of a friend,
Gustave Arosa, a collector, there was this

young banker, passionate, with not much to spend,
but an admirer. Gauguin bought some canvases.

A friendship developed, soon both of them would paint
as he had with Cézanne, both calling him master,

but how to keep joy in his vision innocent
when his heart-shaped palette trembled with disaster?

3

There is something uxorious in Pissarro's landscapes,
as if his brush had made a decorous marriage

with earth's fecundity; her seasons and gates,
the snow-streaked mud of fabrics whose soft cage

held Vuillard and Bonnard in the speckled interiors
of the bourgeois sublime, wine, linen, bread, and flowers;

every framed landscape that he loves in Pontoise
is framed by an open window in its Book of Hours,

compared to the anger in his friend Cézanne, whose
canvas rants at the subject it has chosen, a rage

that builds with a monody grown private and morose
with the obsession of a diary on every page,

the brush muttering imprecations even to a still life
that develops a taciturn distance from his body,

that makes a flower vase no less than his wife,
and repetition the genius of monody,

stroke next to stroke. Narrative excess
had made theatrical melodrama of great art,

but no Pissarro landscape has some rain-whipped wretch
huddling under an oak; he has a balanced heart

without the rhetoric of Delacroix or Turner, wind
silvering the poplars hid whatever wound

he endured raw as a stone quarry, ground
that common shoes walk on, peace that is earned.

Because these virtues grow with the acceleration
of time and the long shadows, because we hoard

what others mocked as safety, in moderation
of self, of fame, the art of being bored

diminishes conceit, and cherishes the plain
and the repetitive: light in a kitchen,

cats coiled on chairs, and sunlight shot with rain,
things without grandeur in their modest shine.

Monchy at dusk or leafy La Feuillée,
so the road, the grazing pastures, especially,

mean more than an avenue's sepulchral grey;
his Paris has that insular intimacy.

As for Pontoise, and its flecked kitchen gardens,
its stalks and peasant girls in spotted scarves,

its talkative aspens, in their providence,
sound like the vendors on old island wharves.

Smoke hangs above a field, across roofs, it has burned
from the day that he painted it, and when it blurs

a pasture where cows graze, unalarmed, everything concurs
with his choice of light, a man urging his cows

across streaked grass, and now both scenes are ours,
the real light and the held, roads flecked with flowers.

So when I look at the Sophoclean shawls
of breakers in late afternoon and smell their salt,

from a hole in the heart, a ground dove calls,
and the poplars of Pontoise sway against cobalt.

His paintings have the meditative progress
of a secular pilgrim, praising its larks and elms,

ricks for their shade, aspens for their light grace,
voluble poplars. Their modesty overwhelms,

their gratitude. Studying his *paysages*
you feel the fevered bliss that shook John Clare

and Edward Thomas, Langland. Whatever the age is,
it lies in the small spring of poetry everywhere.

4

The anger of Courbet and Cézanne made a solid
architecture of quarries and cathedral oaks

hardening the wisps of Corot, so that paint was laid
thick as a plasterer's or a bricklayer's strokes.

The Pointillist surface darts like sardines
in the shallows of the Oise; they shoot like mullet

from the reader's approaching shadow, their darting lines
splinter in bits, not the stoic sculpture of Millet

but the truth of elusive joy, a transient rapture
of hectic strokes that catch the crowds of Paris

scurrying like blown leaves that his brush must capture
before both fade, the shade that sunlight marries.

The thwock of a mattock, the squeak of a barrow's
rusted wheel, of a hay cart rattling a bridge,

or, poked by his brush, a perturbation of swallows
from ricks; sounds at the frame's edge,

and where fanned willows were repeated by the Oise
in its provincial accent, the ochre shallows

reciting their lessons, he has caught the noise
of children's voices gusting through the poplars.

XI

1

This was the light of France: subtler, riper,
ageing, like cheese, the pocked walls of Pontoise,

wide as the aureate wheat in which a reaper
flails with a scythe to raise contentious crows,

abandoned aqueducts, tree-hidden stations,
cloud puffs of steam over a toy-sized train

connecting villages with old hyphenations
and barley, whitening in bright wind, like cane.

These were the hazards of painting *en plein air*:
the dust of the wind and the capricious light

fading and brightening, nowhere was plainer
than his repeated views, none of them right.

There were better landscapes in a restaurant
or on a park's railings. The Salon's choice

omitted him repeatedly. Who would want
300 versions of visions of Pontoise

when Claude would need just one to get it right?
Rejection intensified defiance,

stubborn as Cézanne's stones in the stone light
of L'Estaque, its blue morne in the distance.

So his own canvases stayed as they were,
without narrative pathos, they would insist

on the raw vehemence of real weather,
snow-spattered mud, grey gardens in grey mist.

2

Yet bolts of sadness often shivered him,
like reeds along the Oise occasionally,

when the wind shone it, and swifts would skim
across its light to Charlotte Amalie.

Or when the fogbound barges on the Seine
moored like the schooners of Dronningens Gade,

and every finished canvas he would sign,
despite its skill, made him a little sadder.

As soon as January enters these hills
on the crest of the new year, the breeze brings news

of northern winter storms, the immortelles
ignite their orange flares, and bamboos

shudder like horses' manes; the bells
of lilies silently ring through Santa Cruz,

grass starts to whiten, the dried rut softly
foreshadows drought, an autumn that is ours,

in brittle sticks and yellow leaves and motley
whose strokes echo October in Pontoise;

not that our time has envy of far seasons,
the hills of colours, or that the flame trees' embers

glow with inferior fire, just that our sun's
unceasing glory through ghostly Decembers

consumes the core of doubt by changelessness,
and that the strokes, vermilion and gold,

of pouis and cocoa are not made any less
by oaks and aspens, history-hallowed, old.

3

These little strokes whose syllables confirm
an altering reality for vision

on the blank page, or the imagined frame
of a crisp canvas, are not just his own.

I shift his biography as he shifted houses
in his landscapes; not walled facts, their essence;

neither the strict topography that was Pontoise's
nor the clear charted contours that were the Seine's;

nor ceilings huge with paradisal glow,
incredibly saffron, bearing those breezy

wing-headed cherubs limned by Tiepolo,
or in that Jewish feast by Veronese.

On the gesso surface light writhed silkily
on emerald sleeves, on the plump satin hose,

but his unfinished sketches leave a sky
of patches where the coarse-grained linen shows.

Ours was another landscape, a new people,
not Oise, where a wind sweeps famous savannahs,

with farms and poplars and a piercing steeple,
but cobalt bays and roads through high bananas.

There was no treachery if he turned his back
on the sun that plunges fissures in the fronds

of the feathery immortelles, on a dirt track
with a horse cart for an equestrian bronze.

There is no history now, only the weather,
day's wheeling light, the rising and setting

seasons: young Spring, with her wet hair
gone grey, the colour of forgetting.

4

I have moved him through a fiction I do not inherit,
blocks of Balzac, arched equestrian marshals,

even its interiors: bottles of blood-dark claret,
a loaf's fallen pillar in Chardin, the hushed halls

of Versailles, incredulous fountains
chattering and brimming with astonishment,

disgorging dolphins; my delight remains
in deprivation, not in banishment,

where the sand hardens into sodden pavements
and palms into the charcoal sticks of lindens,

and laburnum, like Susanna, sheds her raiments
and shakes her yellow hair before the dense

gaze of the trembling alders, with the same
petals as the poui, or where, processionally

in April, the immortelles lift their flame
on the burnt hill of Charlotte Amalie,

or when the barges of the chuckling Seine
ride like its schooners, and the veils of dusk

are drawn across the harbour, and the rain
comes slowly down on chimneys, and a red disc

paves the grey river behind the shallow
bank of whatever district, and a woman's laughter

from a small balcony stabs him like a swallow
stitching a twilight of Venetian taffeta.

BOOK THREE

XII

1

A cloudburst over Paris, the blackening towers
of Notre Dame, a cannon clap of thunder,

and then a bannered army, marching showers
and lightning's ordnance searing the sky asunder.

The sodden countryside, its rusts, dun browns
mired in autumn, no longer fired him;

the sense of distant war across distant towns
beyond Louveciennes, while on the fields' rim,

in thin, muck-spattered woods, yellow leaves flared
the colour of malaria, their bodies stricken

and groaning from gales. It was time they fled.
He watched the witches' broth of the Oise thicken.

The group were split apart. The new war hurt
their comradeship; where the troops fought,

the tilled fields burst into bouquets of dirt.
Wounds and chrysanthemums in *nature-morte*;

clattering up a ridge, heads lowered, bayonets fixed,
or blown like immortelle blossoms against the redoubts

or poppies on a far meadow, blues and reds mixed
in a war with the wind that bore their common shouts.

War was a subject for Meissonier and Delacroix,
his skill was not in such fury, he painted peace

in long-shadowed roads, in the gathering war
of silvery thunderheads; battles would pass.

He and his family escaped to London
along with Monet. Sunsets bled in the Thames

and fog erased its monuments, then the sun
dazzled the Houses of Parliament, drying great elms.

He and Monet toured the museums together.
They grew close in enclosing London, their exile

shared a delight in two masters of weather
who earned a reckless confidence of style,

one, flare and mist and haze, of living air,
no mastery too great to be a learner,

they stood before *The Fighting Téméraire,*
silver-leaved Constables and twilight's Turner.

Triangulation: in his drawing room
my father copies *The Fighting Téméraire.*

He and Monet admire the radiant doom
of the original; all three men revere

the crusted barge, its funnel bannering fire,
its torch guiding the great three-master on

to sink in the infernal asphalt of an empire
turning more spectral, like the mastodon.

They both had horror of the beautiful;
Monet obscured the stately Parliament Houses,

while he lacked signature, all he did was fill,
in foul or fair light, the views that were Pontoise's.

Pink roses opened and froze into Manet.
Sunflowers roared in Vincent's head. The breasts

of copper Tahitian beauties with a tray
of glowing mangoes was Gauguin's seal. His rests

on such anonymous pleasures as the glitter
of aspens in wind, shadows on a rough road.

His own road turned when he received a letter
from a frightened neighbour. He sat down to read.

The neighbour was Emilienne. She had
the beak of a village busybody

poking her nose in everything she heard,
a small black sparrow pecking through ordure,

scuttering through Louveciennes like a bird
gleaning cow patties, but now, thanks to her

hopping and pecking with her little hoard
of truths, she told him all about the war.

"You have lost everything you left at Louveciennes.
There were cartloads of dung in the house. The sheep

were slaughtered in your garden." This made no sense.
"The Prussians caused plenty of havoc." She would keep

whichever of a thousand canvases had survived.
About forty. They made mud mats of the rest.

Boots trampled the paintings like flagstones in mud
in a path to the house where soldiers had installed

a slaughterhouse. The floor was greased with blood.
Nothing would be the way that he recalled.

He would see this for himself when he arrived.
But compared to the pain of others, he was blest.

Staccato chrysanthemums, like bursts of gunfire,
and bodies draped over coiled iron rails

like summer laundry; images of his fear,
the tubes of red like disembowelled entrails,

and the gamboge pus of wounds. Cloud hospitals
and crippled withered branches, clouds

like drifting nuns or nurses down the aisles
of groaning soldiers, then the slow-drawn shrouds.

2

When the fields were swept by a remorseful drizzle
misting the canvas, he thought about the war,

how it had felled tall, generous Bazille,
how chronic dysentery desiccated Renoir.

He laid out the capped tubes quietly, row by row.
This blue was Bazille, these ochres the dead at Verdun,

open-mouthed, coiled in the trenches—this furrow
where artillery flashed and thunder trundled its cannon.

The fate of empires in the fallen column
of a loaf by Chardin, its eaten pith

shares with his work now the memorial calm
of a tilled battlefield, a haystack's monolith,

or a clogged peasant limiting a fire
for the spring planting while the Legions march

with leaves of pennons for the Second Empire,
blue tunics, clouds in regimental starch,

and drumming rain rising behind each ridge.
La Gloire, La Gloire, bayonets like lifted wheat

in the wind, and then, the highest privilege
of all: crows, circling marching meat.

As Melbye was once his master he was now Cézanne's,
who copied and copied his large view of Louveciennes:

both pierced by possession, sunk in the earth of France
as Bazille was, in its sunlit indifference.

Now the furrowed earth makes every *sillon* glint
with mica, like a bay. From the blood-washed root,

Spring stains the memory and shoots its tint
through the trunk's twisted tube, its budding fruit.

Spring prances, a flecked stallion, with its file
of horns and hunters, white hounds on tapestries.

Spring with a clatter of rooks from a battlefield
of burdock over lances of fleurs-de-lys.

These furrows of tank tracks on a shadowy road
on whose verge soldiers stalked, past farmhouse walls

and bending fields from which look! the lark arrowed!
Blood rusting the trenches of Normandy's pastorals

is part of the glory, *L'alouette* in high cloud
over Poitiers and Crecy, no butchery without its Bayeux,

an archery of needles embroidering its shroud,
no massacres without masterpieces to show.

He set out for the fields when the sun broke
like any labourer so his work might grow

en plein air only, not a single stroke
made from the comfort of a studio.

Suddenly all his work revealed itself
as a betrayal, all that he had painted

he saw now with another eye whose health
and clarity remained untainted.

That everything he thought he had achieved,
the way in which he painted lanes and trees

and terraced hills russet and heavy-leaved,
was no more than a Sunday amateur's.

Banish the island from your mind completely,
its zebra patterns of palm light and shade,

the rain-glazed drizzles of Charlotte Amalie,
and the slave voices down Dronningens Gade.

The slaves still practised obeah. Was he cursed
for abandoning the island, with the terror

of work unfinished and his death rehearsed
in every casual accident, not error?

Every dawn he seemed to be drifting
far from that mastery which was his aim,

his peace, his port, Pontoise, their uplifting
curse crippling his lifted arm.

Each canvas looks complete, then flaws
race towards his shoes with the thin snarl

of rats surrounding his bare feet with claws
and dribbling centipedes slid down the wall;

a fluttering of swifts trapped in the ceiling
of Charlotte Amalie at dusk mimicked his thought,

his doubt as desperate as a fruit bat reeling
across the beam, then dropping, a crawling clot.

4

Insomniac, cynical, shaken by panic,
by a gradual rejection of all his work,

by the implacable conviction that he was sick
of his own style, with rage that left him weak,

his panic increases. In bed, he senses
that his brain is crumbling, a dried cake's

crumbs on the pillow dribbling from his ears
that he must brush before his wife awakes.

He rises in the dark to the crusted pane
and rubs it with a palm. He is dazed by debt.

It blurs like his cataract. A malicious rain
hazes Pontoise to an indigo silhouette.

Sharp edges on grey cloud, mouldering eaves
eaten with cold, underlined the age

of every stone, twigs with dun olive leaves,
bent, stick-like figures hurrying on a bridge

whose arc accepted transience, for whom Time,
its days, were leaves and clouds, who moved

through the parenthesis of arches, to a sublime
extinction in the city that they loved.

Scuttering spectres—debt, fear, discontent—
crouched in each corner of his stifling house.

A sick child screaming. Counting every cent
with a wife as fertile as she was morose.

Aha! his mirror smiled: this is what it means
to leave the fading Eden where you were,

its violet flowers, primordial blues and greens,
for the smell of absence on varnished furniture.

The repetition of work preserves his reason.
Hostages to debt, his seven children, his wife's voice,

tired of painting, calls Pontoise their just prison,
bent willows trail their hair into the Oise.

(XIII)

1

The weather worsened. Even the sun looked surly.
He saw a rabbit wandering a dark wood.

If Heaven meant to take Jeanne, his angel, early,
it was Heaven's will: which meant that it was good.

But to continue in conspicuous ambition
whose outward guise is modesty, to conceal

failure's resentment, envy, to set the sun
itself as target was no more unreal

than what might lift her body from his mind,
towards that concentric core whose painted heat

is false yet paradisal, the joy we find
in a Tiepolo ceiling, its clear belief

in faith as colour, like a visible wind
that lifts a seraph as easily as a leaf,

he could not place her in elate ascent
to soundless timbrels, soaring with bare feet.

His sorrow fed by her enraging absence,
his febrile, trembling child, his little rabbit,

he still made light of his leaf-uttering scenes,
whose happiness was now the force of habit.

She was the ransom paid to transience:
a shock of starlings, changing maps of snow,

or autumn dying, not conjugating tense,
but branched and rooted in an eternal now,

and therefore every passing was a leaf,
repetitive by example, from which we learn

nothing, no reason for our grief
if there is none for our happiness, in turn.

2

These were the mutterings he heard in water
that settled in stale eddies, the sound of tears:

"You are not the first father to lose a daughter";
"Many left earlier, in even greener years."

But grief cannot endure any argument,
dry tears keep falling from the blackened bough,

where was his child, his angel, while he bent
over a canvas like a tombstone now?

Was death hidden in sunlight where she played
or where his father, tobacco-bearded, sat

on the swaying patterned carpet of leaf-shade,
like the old doctrine, in black rabbinical hat.

3

When dusk is entering his children's eyes
and his wife lights the big brass lamp for supper,

and the toys darken on the grass, he sees
her, dressed at the door, making it appear

that she has never left him, has never left
the chair he wanted her to wriggle into and sit

with her inseparable doll. She looks bereft,
with her moist eyes. Someone has moved her seat.

4

If you forget, you'll banish her forever
with doll and straw hat to the gate of Heaven.

The steady tension of being held together.
When do you start to break? Sob and give in.

O my striped-dress little model, you surrendered
all your small spirit to your papa's portrait,

your wet brown eyes like pebbles in the brook bed
of the summering Oise! Your gaze stares straight

at him, your murderer and maker, with the petals
of your parted lips, the flushed skin, the yellow straw.

She practises perpetual stillness. She settles
too easily into it as he starts to draw.

He haunted her small room. The bed was made.
Her books neatly shelved. Her tiny dresses kept

demurely on the rack. He often stayed,
smelling the fragrant chaos where she had slept.

A cart, a shadowy road with rusting trees,
an axle's piercing creak; in agony

his hand still lit them. All other gestures
maintained incomprehensibility.

He copied the wet sunlight on the leaves
like his own eyes, glazed, inconsolable,

brown furrows baking in their crust like loaves—
her small chair missing from the dinner table.

But all the light in paint could not restore
her short life ravaged by an unfair fever;

he sensed no other world than what he saw,
he caught no glimpse of some celestial river

other than the chimneys of the humbling Oise
and the soft fog that scarved the hills at morning,

though, inexplicably, aspens with one noise
silvered her name, a joy without a warning.

Death claims more lives than one; it claims
others by sharing, its subtracting grief,

as when the aspens' tongues repeated names
that shared her passing, loud in their belief.

The dusk over Louveciennes was not a heaven
of Tiepolo cherubs; every stroke he made

absorbed her absence; with calm, even
paint he built its blue. This was the way he prayed.

ANNA, 1995
Oil on canvas board, 20″ x 24″

1

Out of the Antillean crater, every ridge
looks at both seas, both worlds: Pontoise–St. Thomas,

and sees both sides, both tenses, like that bridge
formed by a causeway of olive casuarinas.

And here is where my narrative must pause,
my couplets rest, at what remains between us,

not Paris's privilege or clouds over Pontoise,
nor the white hulls and flags of the marinas,

but the same reflections that, from a tree's noise,
arrested him, or as he stared at them,

wavering memories. Again I lift the oars
of this couplet, my craft resumes its theme:

At that point where a river, straining to join the sea,
submerges itself in a sand bank, though its surface

corrugates from the eddying wind, it contentedly
nibbles the mangrove roots (this is Hunter's place).

At high tide in the rainy season they both bear one
into the other, to share the thundering shore

but now the wind-grooved lagoon, ark of the heron
(at dusk so numerous they settle by the score),

is damned by the sand bank to a circular motion
fretful to find release, a union known once

but clouded now by the breaker's white commotion,
compared to the wind-plucked wires that are the pond's.

The ochre shallows of the lagoon reflect
the setting empire of an enormous sky,

its end recorded by a clerical egret
pecking through dead leaves for our history.

2

When, from subsiding water, the bank appears
firm as an axiom, the Antillean isthmus

with draining sand bridges both hemispheres,
balancing, like a scale, both images.

That middle passage, that bridge the bank provides,
is one the submerged memory must negotiate

between the worlds it finds on both its sides,
the Caribbean, the Atlantic with its reeking freight,

the archipelago's bridge. On one side is the healing
of Time measured in ruins, the empires of Europe,

its smoke, its spires, and a gold Tiepolo ceiling
towards which we are hoisted by an invisible rope

that hauls us with Ezekiel into a whirlwind
of roiling clouds and trumpeting seraphim

over this pond, but on the other side of the wind
is what exile altered and banishment made dim:

the still pond and the egrets beating home
through the swamp trees, the mangrove's anchors,

and no more bitterness at the Atlantic foam
hurtling the breakwater; the salt that cures.

3

Mossed ropes of mangrove under the pond's surface,
and the murky reflections of the furrowed lagoon,

with old chains and anchors at its hidden base
contain such terrors that none of them are gone.

A broken windmill here and a crusted cauldron
are our open museum of bondage; they hallow the pond

to a litany that is read by a dragonfly's drone,
to a butterfly's wafer where kneeling waves respond,

until unceasingly there is a great High Mass
of clouds in an echoing cathedral, and Tiepolo's

saints look down from pillars, not this quiet grass,
these watery aisles where the surpliced egret bows.

Dusk burrows into the roots from the egret's scream
as it launches itself across the brightened water;

the fraying banner of the dishevelled stream
reddens the reeds from some invisible slaughter.

I have learnt to regulate devotion here
to the egret's step along the wind-grooved metal

on the mangrove's still pool, where, whitening the air,
the egrets fold their wings like palms and settle.

4

Say this for the numerous, quick-stepping covey
of migratory sanderlings; they are faster than the strokes

that mimic their speed on paper, trying to convey,
by a brush's calligraphy, theirs, or a racket of rooks

from a wheat field, that is, the truth that trembles
in the denial of stasis in the pond, of branches

in a lifting wind, all the motes vision assembles
to set leaf or wave alight, as the canvas dances.

It is a coral sunlight with no echoes,
no gods have gone, no nereids from the coves,

no temple ruins where a goat stumbling goes
through the scorched bush, no flutes, only its doves

repeating, not a lament of absence; in the cored
rocks, riddled with holes, or at their base,

where the pools ripple and the crabs have bored
homes in the sand, no echo, only place.

Out in Roseau's lagoon, its corrugations
rustling like rushes in the mud, lies a wrecked,

rusting freighter. The egret stalks in patience,
its beaked pen stabbing from a questioning head,

through brown shallows muttering old degradations.
History is insult, energy is intellect.

History is that tilted freighter stuck in its sense
of the past, the intellect, an egret's ewer of light,

stabbing a phrase, lifting itself over the sound
of repeated parentheses, the circular prayers

perhaps with an outcry of sorrow over the drowned,
beating its wings, till anger soars into grace.

In the reeds, halberds of begonia flame
in their botanical accent, one pointed flange

folded into the other, at its creole name
flaring even brighter. This once felt strange.

(X V)

1

The empire of naming colonised even the trees,
referred our leaves to their originals;

this was the blight on our minds, a speckled disease.
In the convulsive olives of Van Gogh's Arles,

lime trees tried to be olives they could not become,
not less real than reproductions in a book,

but certainly less hallowed. Reality was riven
by these reproductions, and that blight spread

through every noun, even the names we were given,
the paintings we studied, the books we loved to read.

The gommier in flower did not mimic the dogwood
or snow at the roots of white cedar, or Queen Anne's lace,

an apple orchard, or April's autumnal firewood;
they were, like the breadfruit, true to their sense of place.

That tree! Bow to its dark green, motionless power,
my love, its heart fragrant as baked bread

in grace, in shared communion, it makes us poor
as apostles. In it our history is remembered.

2

The brushwork arranged itself in a local frame;
every landscape seemed to delight in its echo of

DOCTRINE, 1991
Watercolour on paper, 12″ x 16″

its French or Spanish original, down to the name,
the sound preceding its subject; we learnt to love

places to whom their sounds were already given,
as our own names were given, until we became,

in the maps of our faces and places, however riven
our hearts by baptism, the same, yet not the same.

Say *Nuevo Mundo Trace*, beyond Valencia
with its grove of imported pines, expecting the sea

through tufts and needles to confirm my indenture
to the silvery painting in the Carnegie Library.

So too the young painter must have felt in France
that the names he knew were not a contradiction

for an islander but his given inheritance,
as one grew more real and the other hazed into fiction.

3

The brush swirls, loaded from a creamy palette,
and in one long stroke draws drought on an ochre plain,

a white cloud conceals the lark's song, *l'alouette*,
clay tiles and a folded cypress confirm Port of Spain.

What did I know of Spain but the ochre echo
that hung over the roofs of colonial Trinidad,

its rivers and bamboo groves, Manzanilla, Mayaro,
its square map echoing Spain's? What the Genoan did,

fingering our rocks on his rosary, was to seal,
rubbing finger and thumb, the indelible christening

of St. Thomas, Santa Lucia, Trinidad, the unreal
baptism of roofs beaded with rain and glistening.

4

Heat. Scorched boulders. Dust in the rutted roads,
stumbling to the crunch of gravel, clay shards, and shale,

mica or quartz in the sun, dry, papery reeds
of leaves whose hues vie with autumn's. I swore: I shall

get their true tints someday. Time, in its teaching,
will provide the bliss of precision, not botanic truth

or museum postcards but the beat of a brush reaching
into its creamy palette, oranges, ochres; but youth

feels it has the measure of Time, that there is a plot
and metre to Time, structured as if it were fiction,

with a beginning, a middle, and an end, except Time is not
narrative, triumph resolved by ambition,

and Time continues its process even for the masters
whose triumph astonishes us, but they are still learning

with arthritic fingers and shovel-wide beards, their disasters
our masterpieces: Van Gogh and Cézanne. Bushes burning

like books in scorched April, when its shadows are cast as
those on the road to Pontoise with autumn returning.

The balance of haze and detail, the recession of ridges
into a general but delicate indigo, the dashes of roofs

reflected in inaudible water, light under bridges
and, in a road aisled with oaks, a cart's mute hooves,

all gone with his century, gone with the lines of devotion
in larches and rook-losing elms, not totally shattered

by war into glass fragments, but the end of motion,
and no more of Nature demanding to be flattered.

For how, unless blood seals the stones, can congealing mortar
from sacrifice lift a spire and the studded doors

hammered by bolts proclaim their celestial powers?
Compared to the stone-webbed vault, what do we matter?

(XVI)

1

A frame from Pissarro: looking from the village bank
outside Gros Islet, across scorched asphalt towards

red roofs and orange, bush scorched by fire, blank
walls and packed trees, grey smoke from green woods.

Stunned heat of noon. In the shade, tan, silken cows
hide in the thorned acacias. A butterfly staggers.

Stamping their hooves from thirst, small horses drowse
or whinny for water. On parched, ochre headlands, daggers

of agave bristle in primordial defence,
like a cornered monster backed up against the sea.

A mongoose charges dry grass and fades through a fence
faster than an afterthought. Dust rises easily.

Haze of the Harmattan, Sahara haze, memory's haze
from the dried well of Africa, the headland's desert

of riders in swirling burnooses, mixed with the greys
of hills veiled in Algerian dust. We inherit the dirt,

the ground dove's cooing on stones, the acacia's
thorns, and the agave's daggers, they are all ours,

the smoky Sahara horsemen, India's and Asia's
plumed mongoose and crested palm tree, Benin and Pontoise.

We are History's afterthought, as the mongoose races
ahead of its time; in drought we discover our shadows,

our origins that range from the most disparate places,
from the dugouts of Guinea to the Nile's canted dhows.

2

The unblest rituals of preparation.
Running tapwater over paint-crusted cells

then scouring with your thumb until they shine
as white as eggshells, from the braced pencils

next to the paper's stiffened sail, select
the gentlest, the paper has been drenched

bravely, alarmingly; lay it flat or else
it warps from undried pools. Your heart is wrenched

by terror, you float on a wind of fear,
and, if it is, as customary as sunrise

bringing light to the white wave and the cobalt air
over furrowing crests, pray that your narrowed eyes

will not betray you with the old result
of vigorous approximation, not the whole

delight of action, smell, the bracing salt,
the shallows' mesh, whose pattern snared my soul.

A ceiling from Tiepolo: afternoon light will ripen
the sky over Martinique to alchemical gold,

a divided life, drawn by the horizon's hyphen
and no less irresolute as I grow old.

The studio windows are hazed by the wind's salt;
their frames misted by the waves' ceaseless arrival.

I settle before an easel to redeem the fault
that multiplies itself in desperate survival.

Something got lost in my leaves, a precise gaiety
of yellow that exceeds itself in exultant edges,

of delight that dulled into duty, in the umber wedges,
of rocks over lace-light shallows, the frailty

a thread that has broken its invisible anchor,
a canvas whose rudderless sail drifts from its course

to morose resignation, a plodding, monotonous rancour
at a surface that smiles then betrays. The betrayal is yours.

3

More failures stare through their frames, accusing corpses
erect in their coffins, a dead light in their eyes,

as you, their quiet murderer, conduct your own autopsies.
Outside them the ocean is mixing its different dyes.

If I pitched my tints to a rhetorical excess,
it was not from ambition but to touch the sublime,

to heighten the commonplace into the sacredness
of objects made radiant by the slow glaze of time,

from the dark that slices a loaf of bread by Chardin,
powerful as a porous pillar, or a wedge of cheese

monumental in stillness, to light that can gladden
the mind like the flash of a hound's thigh in Veronese.

I approach every canvas with a pompous piety,
faithful to the lines of the drawing, a devotion transferred

GROS ISLET CHURCH I, 1998
Oil on canvas, 18″ x 24″

from a different servitude, to lines of poetry
proceeding by systematic scansion, brushstroke and word.

The painting's surfaces are too gritty, greasy,
not dexterous, yet accurate, more muck-fuss than stipple,

those levitating shadows that the breeze makes easy
running over wild grass and in a rivulet's ripple,

and if these couplets were furrows, the spring fields of Pontoise,
the cool, aspen-relishing wind bending long rows

of corn, grooving the furrows and oval contours
of the tilled hillsides: still, the same sun is yours.

The same windy light in the waves of the Central Plain,
egrets or cloud-schooners crossing a sea of cane,

the same silvering birches of approaching rain,
if this pen were a brush, and a brush as true as your pen.

4

A hollow humming in the heart, charred
like a scorched stump and gnawed in rings,

can make hills rise, or blue smoke from a yard,
or a twisting track. Separation only brings

sharper definition, sun-startled angles
of trunks over a small stream, bright corners

we had not thought preserved, the way that glass
cedes its reflections, or change, as torn as

clouds passing over a forest's face, a shadow
over a road, that is the painful precision

of exile, detail's mound of exact increase,
not as one thought or read, of dimming vision

by distance, but its opposite. The trees
I never thought I needed to remember, bush

or charred trunk against the changing sea's
hues and channels, eluding pen and brush.

Running on the high sea road the gamboge cliffs
nearing Micoud in April, the whole ocean

widening in the wind, the gloricidia's leaves
silvery fluttering. O so much benediction!

Devour the last crumbs of Time, crusts and leftovers,
like the curved wolfhound at Tiepolo's feast,

glad for a privilege, before the embroidered covers
are folded and the waves' timbrels have ceased.

(**XVII**)

1

The nation was in an uproar, in his quiet place
the rumour besieged his windows, the starlings rose,

adding clamorous opinions to the Dreyfus case
over the chimney cannons and the trenches of Pontoise.

Dreyfus was the subject of Emile Zola's *J'Accuse,*
Zola claiming the army had falsified evidence;

he shared the blood hatred, the family circumstance,
the Sephardic separation, it cut to the bone.

The fields, the small farms, were they a separate France
as they were for Dreyfus, his birthplace, never their own?

He wasn't much of a Jew. He did not observe,
as he had on the island, the tribal sorrow

that Dreyfus added to. How could he serve
the fields of France with a name like Pissarro,

his brush that he surrendered, hilt reversed,
his sword snapped like a pencil on the knee,

his revers stripped, because his tribe was cursed,
a nation separate in its treachery?

2

My inexact and blurred biography
is like his painting; that is fiction's treason,

to deny fact, alter topography
to its own map; he too had his reason

for being false to France. Conspirators, spies
are what all artists are, changing the truth;

as much a traitor in his comrades' eyes
as the brisk officer; his work was proof.

The minute the traitor Dreyfus was condemned
he ceased being a Frenchman, a Jew.

That is what it boiled down to in the end.
That is what mattered, that's why it was true.

Thus all his canvases were forgeries
the way that Dreyfus copied his own script

with false mistakes, strokes that were subtle lies,
keeping those errors where his brush had slipped

to make a sworn treachery of Art
as Dreyfus had of service. Clemenceau's curse:

"Nothing but an obscene soul and an abject heart."
Perhaps of either treachery Art was worse.

Perhaps his brushstrokes should have been subjected
to their analysis, as was Dreyfus's hand.

Examined closely, his foliage could be read
as Hebrew script; each vowel, each ampersand.

Had he not copied with Sephardic eyes
those fields, those *sillons* where her workers bled

with that exact delight with which a spy's
hypocrisy reported truth, the faith he shared

with that vile captain of artillery
who knew his accuracy would be rewarded

by haters of his tribe? And what was he,
a Jew, doing in officer class? The case was sordid.

The case exploded into shattering glass.
In Nantes, three thousand marchers screamed one threat.

In Nancy, no worshippers dared pass
their besieged synagogue, far less enter it.

This was not the Synagogue of Peace and Loving Deeds
close to Dronningens Street by the blue water;

no, this was Europe; this is where the seeds
are sown in shattered crystal of slow slaughter.

Now he kept dreaming of a yellow wall,
its surface scratched with slogans, in some part

of a very old city, in, perhaps, Portugal,
with a bell clanging and bodies on a cart.

A cart heaped, not with firewood, but with stiff
corpses, without branches or limbs,

nailed with a crudely painted board: LES JUIFS,
like a medieval woodcut, then, that dims.

The bell's clangour, close, cold, then fading
through the infecting streets became the sound

of a church's clapper along Dronningens Gade.
Then the auction bell. Slaves huddled on hot sand

and the names of his family being called out
by the ragged bellman, "*Peste!*" The plague

was his own skin and colour; then they were brought
to the edge of a wharf, in light both clear and vague.

Such a light as comes off old maps: of pearl,
of bone, of ivory, with the pallor of Time

from the Torah, the pates of rabbis; they appeal
to something sallow and subdued in him,

not the alternating pogroms of rain and heat,
and their hot shadows, all the months long,

whose horror was a hound crossing the street
dragging its shadow with an orange tongue.

3

The Synagogue of Blessing and Peace and Loving Deeds
and the slave hymn from Charlotte Amalie's wharf,

the beards of the Elders sprinkled with the seeds
of a desert faith. Painting was not enough.

Yet it is for him the surest benediction
as the seasons sweep past, still his inheritance

even if his canvases endorsed the fiction
that its citizens believed, an equal France.

And equally, each internecine nation
outside the museums with their marching crowds

in the flags of Bastille Day, their separation
at the peak of summer's joy, till one wrist broods

on its singed number, on the Dreyfus affair,
and a smoking chimney predicts his origins,

the peaked candles of brushes in the Seder
of an attic, a smoke wreath from the ovens.

Yet he copies the congealed marbles of Fiorenza,
contorted statuary and the mortuary drains

of Venice, his art entangled in the frenzy
of naiads and dolphins in disgorging fountains.

France had always been his, despite his birthplace,
the light of the islands was slowly being lost

at dusk on the sallow skin of his different race,
with the scent of salt. Transparent as a ghost,

the pain of being provincial was a scab, the badge
of his unsettled heart, doubt fills his head

with the privilege of echoing rotundas, a famous bridge,
galleries that punished him, the great books unread,

huge frescoes with ecstasies of precision,
their delight in balance, of stallions floating

and trumpeting seraphs, the terror of tradition;
and from their balustrade, Tiepolo and Veronese gloating.

Dreyfus was sentenced to his own paradise—
the Caribbean, off the coast of Cayenne,

on Devil's Island, where, if he dies, he dies
in sea and sunshine, luckier than most men.

In cool October, under a pink sky,
a cold grey street with quiet trees and roofs,

the sunrise, occupying Germany,
stirs the dead leaves in whispers. Nothing moves.

Their history, their light are not for you.
Their autumn blazes with the astonishment

of dispossession, if you were a Jew,
and wore the yellow leaf of banishment.

Silver coins in the leaves of Wolfenbüttel.
The Jew is our burden. The ramrod stance

and spectacled stare, his oath as brittle
as a snapped sword. Dreyfus. Jewdas of France.

Winter comes racing, a hound in icicled coat,
its orange thigh flaring like a flame in snow,

in the crisp slopes of Bruegel wooden rooks float
over bowed hunters, heads lowered as they go.

The season comes with black strokes and chestnut fires
in pavement braziers, wet wriggles for a tree's limbs,

with piebald yards and roofs and village spires
erasing themselves in the fog. His brushes freeze.

The stove starry with spitting logs, the fires
of a night sky that is Charlotte Amalie's.

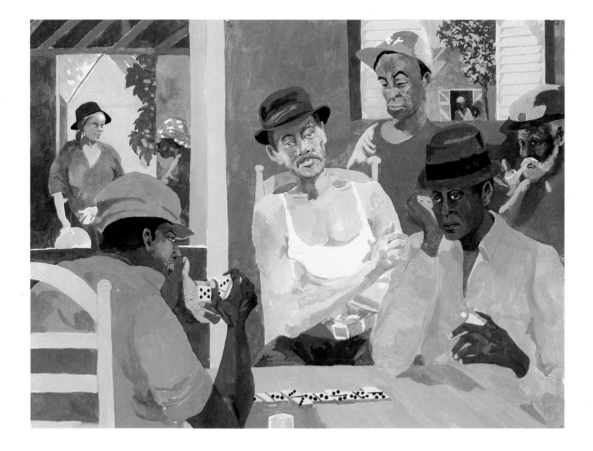

(XVIII)

1

Storks nest again in the tower of Alcalá;
from Spain, our names, music, a language's shapes,

white walls, tiled roofs, a light the same colour
as summer in Madrid, huge clouds like crossing ships.

Olives of Granada. Looking out from the car:
bulls stood on their shadows like trampled capes.

Then standing over the quarry where they shot Lorca:
vine sticks like rifles, the clot of ruby grapes.

Hot walls of Spain. An outburst of bougainvillea
along a dry road in real, dusty Valencia.

Arches of echoes. In hot leaves I could hear
hidden streams in the stones, my friendship's indenture

to Michael and John, beneficiary of their wills,
from the quill of an egret in the feathering reeds;

their names are entered in the lines of the brown hills,
in the annals of blue mountains along its red roads,

and blue cloud absorbs the lark's song: "*Alouette,*"
clay tiles and a folded cypress outside Port of Spain,

and Michael's cackle still comes when I least expect,
and John Hearne's voice, driving towards Blue Mountain,

"*Los Quatros Generales,*" on the pine breeze
"Madrid, your tears of sorrow," to Oracabessa

over Junction Road and Newcastle, not the Pyrenees,
but equally loved, none greater or lesser,

loved by J. Figueroa, pate and beard like Pissarro's,
Sephardic Jamaica, his pain San Juan de la Cruz,

all friends and princes, their loss like small arrows
that pierce the mind, sparrows over Pontoise.

They were natural men, their lilting conversation
carried melody and intelligence, though they were torn

by the imperial echoes of their island nation
in its parched mountains, rooted where they were born.

See: Gauguin's portrait of Camille Pissarro.
Pencil. 1880. Bald head, glasses, the thick nose,

Sephardic Caribbean. See: John Figueroa.
Lover of France. Dead dear friend. The lark arrows.

See also the cloudy rabbinical beard,
sunbeam skating his baldness, the gaze

alert with mischief, and a fierce, inbred,
and rancorous temper; Sephardic Portuguese,

but his faith Veronese's and Tiepolo's
from font to ceiling, like a minor saint

with lifted fingers under the stone rose
of a stained window, flesh becoming paint.

2

They felt the climate of devotion grow
from the red clay and fringed pines of the mountains,

the indigo ridges cloud-streaked as if snow
blew from the Pyrenees and the view were Spain's

not just Newcastle, where the English camp
swung arms to orders in some shire's accent,

the drumming ground doubling the regiment's stamp
and echoing HALT! Halt: but to the scent

of mountain lilies on cold, plunging slopes
where they grow coffee and wild strawberries,

and where the nightingales repeat the hopes
they have learnt from poetry that the owl queries.

Their devotion grew the way that mountain grass
grew over a bare field where blackbirds raced

after the drought, where lambs and kids still graze
and buck with joy; it was securely placed

in the names it knew, permanent
as the pain from which it came; it was just

in its anguish, its farewell to the regiment,
the shouts and drums, and slowly, the fading dust.

The dusk fades, unchanged, the ranks of pines
and plume-stirring conifers come to attention

and echo Aragon or the blurred outlines
of a fogbound shire, in the far ascension

of rooks or John-crows over a wet crag
where a stream signals its mirror in the sun.

There are veins that carry, like the mountain brooks
down Gordon Town, Newcastle, strange with pines,

those friends whose breath has faded into books
that pierce your heart like the old roadside signs

to Stony Hill, and over the coiling corners
into the gusting pastures of Saint Ann's

and a herd of horses grazing, quiet mourners
in the bright sun-shot grass, down all the islands

from the Virgins to that Sunday where a dog
crossed the stunned street, when the clouds move

over the Savannah, like a catalogue
of early Pissarro, harbours hazed with love.

3

The incredible blue with its bird-enfolding cloud,
in which there are crumbling towers, banners, and domes,

the crumbling Carthage of sunsets, the canvas shroud
drawn over associations that were Greece's and Rome's

but rarely of Africa. They continue at sixty-seven
to echo in the corridors of the head, perspectives

of a corridor in the Vatican that led, not to Heaven,
but to more paintings of Heaven, ideas in sieves

drained by satiety, because great art can exhaust us,
and even the steadiest faith can be clogged by excess,

the self-assured Christs, the Madonnas' inflexible postures.
The hound raced with my thought to brightening Venice.

Here a black mongrel, nosing around a bright boat,
is chased, then chased again, but has returned

without any shame; turn your gaze about
to the starved pot hound that your foot once spurned.

4

The shadows lengthen, regular as their dial—
spring in Pontoise, autumn in Louveciennes,

dawn in Dronningens Street, dusk down an aisle
of palms or poplars as each season ends

with spindly legs, wet eyes, and wheezing breath,
like an old, moulting heron in the reeds

stabbing at sprats and tadpoles scurrying beneath
the cold pond's surface, and the grassy seeds

of the feathery sedge, bent, growing older,
with a hand adept and resolute, the years pass,

bringing more bending pains in his right shoulder,
blending a grey heron in the rusted grass.

Here, in the zinc-white wriggles of the marina,
the yachts cluster, close as egrets feeding,

the orange roofs brighten, the low hills greener—
then the rough hills beyond with their receding

indigos and often the ochre scars
of garden clearings and the flash of walls

through screening trees, the poplars of Pontoise,
or the sail-crowded Seine, and when dusk falls

on the glittering coined lagoon, its ropes
in wobbling water, a landing stage

looming like Venice, where one traveller hopes
his search will close a vaporetto's passage.

BOOK FOUR

(**X I X**)

1

The backfiring engine of the vaporetto
scumbled the reflections of her palaces,

the wake braided its hair; now I would get to
the roaring feast with its fork-bearded faces.

The emerald sleeve of the immense lagoon
shone on a wriggling wall where she would turn

from the pearl drops on her embroidered gown,
while water lapped the landing with its tongue.

A gondola's crescent shell, the quarter-moon,
slid with its delving prow dividing coin

minted at sunrise, melting the lagoon
with alchemy where sky and water join.

Through some canal's embroidery, I thought,
I'll trace the thread that carries memory

back to the original, where one stroke caught
the bright vermilion of the white hound's thigh.

Behind these lace palazzos was the work
that chance had brought me closer to; aboard

the lace perspective widening in the wake
of the warping ferry, my hope was restored

that, in the mesh of sunlight which was Venice,
whose gulls on pilings mimicked the standards

of the Doge's galleons (proving that empires vanish
while water has one tense and cannot run backwards)

from a small colony with no book for a guide,
I would discover in some flaking church,

with peering pilgrims scuffling inside
water-webbed walls, the creature of my search.

I sat in the small square, trying to control
a sense of swaying on its grid of stone.

Guardi passed, gliding in a gondola.
To walk in Venice seemed a contradiction.

Benches and flagstones were moored in water
on either side, creaking awnings

were a slow barge's sails. I arrived after
my body, as from a boat. Mornings

lit a red wall whose window framed a terrace,
set with white tables in a bower of grapes;

my gestures occupied a painted space
in the carved orb that Saint Mark's lion grips.

A flag's cheeks filled with wind. Light shaped the square.
A strenuous fountain failed to touch the sky.

Pigeons exploded, darkening the bright air,
and settled on a bridge, short as a sigh.

One block from our small brown pensione were
frescoes of the Veronese museum, the stage

where he too disembarked, ignored, to enter
with gaping tourists in his own pilgrimage.

What was this strange transaction, what bronze horse
arched over a square's traffic was my own

imagination's envy? Was Venice's force
a slow surrendering, an astonished groan

at irresistible light, at water writing
reflections, signatures, no more denying

my joy in the pigeon-alighting
piazza, the column's pawing lion?

The rainbow oils in wobbling canals
off the lagoon's wide stretch whose stench is

as legendary as its pastel walls
and ornate landings, the festering Venice

I was prepared for was an odourless light
wavering from painted moorings like a net,

till all that splendour tired with its delight,
glazed as a fresco with its spray, still wet.

Venice was both itself and a catalogue
of reproductions, but I had lost the page

in that book of Craven's where the spectral dog
haunted dark hose, and I felt the old rage

at my stubborn uncertainty. Research
could prove the hound Tiepolo's or Veronese's

but I refused. Faith was a closed church
like my old TREASURY OF ART MASTERPIECES.

Fugitive Tiepolo! Shadows and short streets.
Ducking through fleets of laundry, past the prows

of the lagoon's traffic, through stench that sits
on the stagnant canals, their stones bearded with moss.

A poling shallop carries him across
to the other mooring with its mast-filled sky,

they nearly caught him in the carnal house
last night. Her wild hair, her pliant thigh.

It always happened. With every sunrise
he was stunned by a beauty he had seen before

so far beyond nature in her artifice
he loved her with everything he could offer,

riding on her own scum, bejewelled Venice,
studded with tributary gems, a radiant whore

steeped in the secular luxury of vice,
incalculable pearls in her bright hair,

stretching her hand to feed an arching hound,
lap-lap, lick-lick, like the obeisant water

slurping the prow, the steady, obscene sound
of a dog's tongue lapping a pewter saucer.

Separated by two centuries, my two Venetians,
Verona's Veronese, each rendered taffeta,

pleated and peaked, differently. The older one's
affability with angels, the clear eye of the other.

GROS ISLET CHURCH II, 1999
Oil on canvas, 16″ x 20″

Tiepolo was shields and mirrors, dusk on a cedar,
rose-tinted precipices, lifting sails, lilac seas, the

operatic *Rinaldo Taking Leave of Armida,*
so the phantom wolfhound was surely by Veronese.

Her bronze hair's hammered coil, its fiery glint
catching the sunset's grate; here is Rinaldo,

his skin flushed with sunset, in the Phaidon print
the light flares, dyeing his armoured shoulder.

In that pose of immobile departure, I hold the page
to the ageing light as my own hand grows older;

they are eternally fixed, age after age,
and it is I who fade, dimming beholder.

3

Since that book of prints I had carried in my head,
the saffron ceiling of my skull's rotunda,

with the soles of martyrs ascending in parted
clouds in radiant conversion, but for this wanderer

only a spectre counted: the hunched phantom
at the feast's surfeit, not saints possessed

by their own radiance. Should the hound come
nibbling my hand's wafer, it would be blest.

But I felt that had I stalked it, the spectral dog
would hide in a forest of hose, peering behind

the folded dog's ear of a catalogue
then bolting off, catching my scent upwind,

I moved her image as one might a chess piece,
looking over her emerald sleeve with parted lips,

the white wolf, eyes slits, nudging her knees,
the windowed ruby glass from which she sips.

The wolfhound skinned its teeth in a sneering curse
as I approached the wall. I was there alone,

my shadow joined the feast, then on the fresco's
wall a door opened and the dog was gone.

4

The white dog turned and leapt from the fresco
to trot, head nodding, through a shadowy scene:

a lapping canal, leaving the echo
of a white silhouette where it had been,

as if its outline had been drawn in error
to be repainted by its maker's hand

crouched in a doorway, where, a spectral terror,
it guarded memory like a real hound.

What if at the maze's end I did not encounter
the hound, in profile and graceful in its arc,

with its brightened thigh? At least I could recount the
flame that had led me, a tongue in the dark,

as the lamp of Eurydice's hair led Orpheus
to Mercury's whispering winged feet through the gloom

or, better still, in the Morne's deepening dusk,
a palm shields a match and a lamp warms a room?

The growing cloud of doubt gathered its pace
across intellectual brightness, dyslexic fog

furred and obscured the edge of a fresco's surface,
was I scared to death to find this bone-white dog?

Devoted as a candle to its church,
the thigh flared steadily, more affliction

than quest now, I would end my search,
if faith were just the fiction of a fiction.

The dog was ageless, not I, its beholder
in the shuffling crowd. Was I afraid to meet

my white-haired love, looking over her shoulder,
paused on a marble couplet at the Met?

Cowardice, stubbornness, indifference
made too much of the whiteness of the hound,

whose reproduction in some book of prints
of sacred frescoes I have never found,

until I doubt the very beast's existence
as much as mine sometimes, like the white sound

made by a snowfall on a winter fence,
the thunder of my shadow on white sand.

Preserve it with the details of a dream,
as in a dream, the roaring, voiceless feast,

white hand, white hound, as I remembered them,
Dominis Canae, the rechristened beast!

Why at the House of Levi, though, unless
in all the autumnal riot of the house,

Sephardic guests in silvery coined Venice
were welcome then, and a few turbanned Moors?

His reputation on a dagger's point,
Jealousy's swirling cloak and Envy's ambush

in liquid alleys only brightened his paint
despite these dangers, what came from his brush?

A feast to flatter one luxurious Jew
who paved his acclamation with new coin

like sunrise on the square, with crumbs he threw
to applauding pigeons, seasoned in their scorn.

This vast, blasphemous fresco! Hasn't he learnt
from the foul-mouthed canals of his disgrace,

to comport himself? This dish of water meant
for a lapping hound, flung in the Church's face?

The visitor to Venice becomes a student of water
and its biography, which is life made easy

by gossip. I heard this later
from waves that whispered: *Paolo Caliari Veronese,*

a sculptor's son, was for Feast in the House of Levi
charged by the Inquisition for irreverence.

Too Semitic in his symmetry? Who knows? I
saw a white crow's mask on the face of Venice.

Painting releases our benign surprise
at a coal face, while we take a white hound

for granted, but what if among Three Magis
in the rush manger one lifts a black hand?

PRIORY AT GROS ISLET, 1999

Oil on canvas, 16″ x 20″

(**XX**)

1

Over the years the feast's details grew fainter,
less urgent, and with it this: I could not recall

my first love's features; memory was my painter,
but her gold-haired figure rose and left its wall.

She had become as spectral as the hound,
a paint-thin phantom of real flesh and voice

on a flaking wall; but time has always found
ways to erase the outlines of our joys.

Paint would preserve her white wax hand that fed
the hound, the light on her rich sleeve, but she,

whom my young adoration once compared
to the fresco's replica, had moved away from me.

The dying light will alchemise the harbour,
whiten the schooners' hulls, and the immense

clouds change their ceiling on bright water.
She lives in paint that cannot change its tense.

Was the name Tiepolo there for euphony?
No skill in the depiction of the beast

ageless, perfection, any one of the
two names might have done it; who painted it best

was not at issue, mastery grew easy,
but where I first beheld the spectral hound.

I would say Veronese for Ver-o-nes-e,
I heard the echo and took it for the sound.

Over the years the arc of the lost hound
faded further; its phantom had appeared

when I, mounting the stairs of these couplets, found
the frame of memory again, but its rust never cleared.

It faded like a pattern Time unstitched
from a hunting tapestry, like a daylight owl.

Was the white beast old age or only a long-wished-
for death, or simply the transparent soul?

2

I ravaged a volume on Tiepolo later.
I was searching for myself now, and I found

The Meeting of Antony and Cleopatra,
I was that grey Moor clutching a wolfhound,

tan and excitable the dog frets at her,
the Queen gliding in jewels and her train.

Venice is dimming, her diadems in eclipse,
her fleet foundering at Actium, once again

the pages turn their sails, this time: *The Banquet
of Antony and Cleopatra.* Here the Queen

poises a pearl over a goblet; in the quiet,
a Moor in a doublet and brown hound frame the scene.

This was something I had not seen before,
since every figure lent the light perfection,

that every hound had its attendant Moor
restraining it with dutiful affection.

I riffled through the derisive catalogue
determined that the fact was not a vision.

(The dog, the dog, where was the fucking dog?)
Their postures wrong. Nothing confirmed my version.

The prints confirmed his debt to Veronese,
his distant master; tiringly inspired,

he learnt from him to keep his gestures busy
and the light clear; by now he has acquired

the weight and flourish of a public syntax
Veron-easy with colloquial scholarship,

the repetition of deep-fissured backs
and saffron clouds bearing their Virgin up.

Enormous banners gusting in the wind,
golden clouds lift the apostolic host,

their postures born from Veronese's mind,
he is their shaper, their instructive ghost.

Bright-bellied stallions neigh, and chariots
stir tinted smoke, not dust, their pawing hooves

trample the light, the bright rotunda riots
with fury that is motionless but moves.

O turbulence, astounding in its stasis;
O bright and paradisal wind conveying

the swirl of robes, the light-uplifted faces
to the clouds' core, ascending and yet staying

with their bare soles as if their legion spun
like leaves in an autumn gust, but noiselessly,

a saffron glow, not from our mortal sun
that sets and rises, shadowless ecstasy

ordained, we understand that orthodox
depiction, but joy carries it away

to weightless grace, the way a pilgrim walks
on cloud-paths to the Holy Family.

3

They evolve via Veronese, his
bodies that tumble in bright buoyancy

and lift above cloud-chasmed crevices,
their robes in a vertiginous argosy,

his *putti*, light and smooth as bubbles blown
by a saffron wind; it is always late

afternoon in his paradise, in the blest stone
bay of a ceiling busy with its freight;

Venice inverted, hectic with the sails
of crossing saints and, above them, the Star

of the coined water, weighed in her scales
commerce and faith, money and mystery.

Dante in paint, but not quite paradise; yet
there is a fixed sublime in Tiepolo,

whose light is always a little before sunset,
a sweet dissolving like high summer snow,

a vision so acclimatised to faith
and orthodoxy that when we look on her

we see a breathless beauty without breath,
the Infant-cradling, cloud-enthroned Madonna.

4

I had followed in the footprints of the hound,
and not the hound my shadow, the hound was white,

if that were all, then nothing had been found.
It stands as still as when he painted it.

I still believe its phantom and the event
that, from apprenticeship, led me so far,

when the bright startling thigh before me went
like its own candle, separate, secular.

Where had it led me, the desperate, tenuous claim,
the thread that kept its labyrinthine course

through the brocaded channels whose jewels flame
when sunrise strikes the water with such force?

To History, a bellowing Minotaur
pursued and slain, following, as termites do,

these furrowing tunnels, couplets to where
this mixed obscenity made by the two

coupling worlds, a beast in the shaft
of light, trampled its filth, a beast

that was my fear, my self, my craft,
not the white elegant wolfhound at the feast.

If recognition was the grace I needed
to elevate my race from its foul lair

by prayer, by poetry, by couplets repeated
over its carcase, I was both slain and slayer.

Time swung its pendulum's axe through any weather,
it swayed inside my heart. I heard it where

the dial stared, then brought its palms together
at noon and midnight in a steepled prayer.

SAVANNAH GALLOP: PORT OF SPAIN, 1985
Watercolour on paper, 12½″ x 16″
Mr. & Mrs. Colvin Chen

(**XXI**)

1

Blessed Mary of the Derelicts. The church in Venice,
painted at nineteen, confirms the arch he spanned,

the hound's progenitor, the young Veronese;
a fresco's page arrests my halting hand

but none holds in its frame the arching dog
that has become spectral, a vision

loosened from its epoch; the rustling catalogue
whispers Veronese, but here, as contradiction,

is another print! *Apelles Painting Campaspe*
is this allegory Tiepolo has painted himself,

painting his costumed models, on the floor, what must be
his mascot: a white lapdog revels in the wealth

of Venetian light. Alexander sprawls in a chair.
An admiring African peers from the canvas's edge

where a bare-shouldered model, Campaspe with gold hair,
sees her myth evolve. The Moor silent with privilege.

If the frame is Time, with the usual saffron burning
of his ceilings over which robed figures glide,

we presume from the African's posture that I too am learning
both skill and conversion watching from the painting's side.

Santa Maria del Rosario, Sant'Alvise,
Santa Maria della Visitazione, formal research

recites his ceilings in Italy, as faith raises the
scaffold of Giambattista Tiepolo in an island church,

his figure receding in the lifted devotion
of fishermen who cross themselves with salted eyes

as he climbs to his crow's nest above the muttering ocean
of vespers to chart the geography of paradise.

Each rusting village acknowledged her dominion,
Star of the Sea, from its dark, echoing nave,

her canoes genuflecting for Communion
before the lace-fringed altar of a wave.

Each reproduction, even in monochrome,
fresco or ceiling in a pale ochre wash,

made the world through its window one with Rome,
her sceptre a cane stalk, her orb a calabash.

The cult and elevation of the Virgin
through roiling, soundless cloud was not my own

upbringing, far less his, and yet conversion
of a kind came with the echoing stone

cupolas, frescoes, banners, and ceilings, the same
ceremonies of Communion, the Mass in Latin,

even in hovels with their struggling flame
to the Madonna, and the throne she sat in.

And the beads of islands, bedded like the seeds
of a sugar apple in their pith of foam,

from the Synagogue of Blessing and Peace and Loving Deeds
to the black chapels where our songs came from.

Volumes of turning cloud in a conch-shell sky,
a floating Madonna, putti with ears like wings,

over tin and blackened shingles the squat belfry
of Anse La Raye divides us when it rings,

and a sky in rose and gold confirms the harmony
of a single faith, trunks with broad breadfruit leaves

to the scrolled palm-pillars of the Scuola dei Carmini,
the watery light pearled on the Virgin's sleeves,

the bright stroke on a mongrel scavenging sand
before dark on the fading beach of Canaries,

the light in the dog's thigh made by the sun's hand,
as it turns and fills its outline in a masterpiece.

3

Garnet-eyed and gazing towards Zion,
a settlement of Abyssinian apostles,

bearded as smoke, have founded a religion
based on the horizon, while the old one jostles

for space in the old cathedral. Garbage in drains,
the furnace that rules the village by its stasis.

They have designed themselves so that what remains
is the Coptic fantasy in their stoned faces.

They have designed their faith, with leonine
locks, some shaggy with rust, till, in repose,

banners and beards are one in their design,
figures not Veronese's or Tiepolo's.

They have not seen Dürer's panels: Four Apostles,
not the Moorish princes of the Renaissance,

they echo a blue altarpiece in their postures,
one turbanned soldier with a bamboo lance.

On the beach a young tourist with her head inclined
towards an infant she cradles in her arms

is a Fra Angelico in a blue wraparound, as the wind
begins the incantations of pliable palms;

everywhere a craft confirming images,
from a nosing mongrel to a challenging ceiling

of cloud. The mind raised on mirages
sees my father's copy of storm gulls wheeling.

4

Vessel, apprentice and interpreter,
my own delight, before the frames of Time,

was innocent, ignorant and corruptible,
monodic as our climate in its sublime

indifference to seasonal modulations,
to schools, to epochs; I had read them, yes,

but art was not an index of elations;
it ignored error, it trusted its own eyes.

PASTURE, DRY SEASON, 1998
Oil on canvas board, 18″ x 26″

The hound's thigh blurred the smoky dyes around it,
it mixed the schools of distinct centuries,

fixed in its stance it stays where I had found it,
painted by both, Tiepolo, Veronese;

since what is crucial was not true ascription
to either hand—rather the consequence

of my astonishment, which has blent this fiction
to what is true without a change of tense.

Not that Time in a larger frame might have shown the gift
I believed in, and something more astonishing might

have resulted in paint, when on a cloud's wall swift
birds dart over it like a brush's flight

over a causeway with feathery branches, as azaleas
blaze in a vase like that canvas with its zinc glare

in my first Cézanne. He too was crazed by failures,
you can see the gleam of a madman in his stare.

My father's bones in my wrist, in the white Easter
linen of a crucified canvas nailed for his sons—

Lucien, son of Camille, Domenico of Giambattista,
from hand to veined hand the gift, from example, inheritance.

Ah, the hyphen of unfinished things, the unachieved—
like that shaft of light in the fading sky, the lance

of a brush crossing the canvas! O loss, that believed
in Time and its talent! The racing shadows advance.

1

One dawn I woke up to the gradual terror
that all I had written of the hound was false.

I had pursued a melody of error,
my craft seduced by the twin siren calls

of Memory changing to Imagination,
of Reason into Rhyme. I knew I stood

before the uproar of a feast. Its station
was Venice, unvisited. Its poles were my dark wood,

from which the hound, now a chained Cerberus, growled
and lunged its treble heads at Accuracy,

a simple fact made myth, and the myth fouled
by its demonic piss. Tiepolo, Veronese,

the image I had cherished made no sense,
my memory's transference of their frescoes

meant that I never learnt the difference
between Veronese's gift and Tiepolo's.

And yet I hold my ground and hold it till
I trace the evasive hound beyond my fear

that it never existed, that exhaustion will
claim action as illusion, from despair.

Because if both Venetians painted frescoes,
then what I thought I saw had to be panels

or canvas seamed, but still the image grows
with more conviction there and nowhere else.

Then how could I be standing in two places,
first, in a Venice I had never seen,

despite its sharpness of prong-bearded faces,
then at the Metropolitan? What did the dog mean?

2

Over the years I abandoned the claim
of a passion which, if it existed, naturally faded

from my island Pissarro, rooted in his fame,
a smoke wisp on the Seine, his exile dictated

by a fiction that sought from him discipleship
in light and affection for our shacks and ridges

touched by crepuscular orange. No black steamship
roiled in its wake a pain that was ever his;

no loss of St. Thomas. Our characters are blent
not by talent but by climate and calling. Cézanne's

signing his work, *Pupil of Pissarro*, all I meant
was only affection's homage, and affection's

envy, benign as dusk arching over Charlotte Amalie,
and night, when centuries vanish, or when dawns rise

on the golden alleys of Paris, Castries, or Italy,
ceilings of Tiepolo or Veronese in changing skies.

A change of Muses, a change of light and customs,
of crooked tracks for avenues of bricks for straw,

change fiddling orchestras for firelit drums,
they were never his people, we were there to draw.

They, and everything else. Our native grace
is still a backward bending, out of fashion

in theatres and galleries; an island race
damned to the provincialities of passion.

My Muses pass, in their earth-rooted stride,
basket-balancing illiterate women, their load

an earthen vessel, its springs of joy inside,
pliant shadows striding down a mountain road.

In evening light a frangipani's antlers
darken over spume crests and become invisible

even to the full moon, and as dusk always does
for my eyes, and his lights bud on the black hill

to a cobbled brook's tireless recitation
in voluble pebbles as lucent as the ones

under the soles of the Baptist. Morning sun
on the corrugating stream over clean stones.

3

I thoroughly understand all he endures:
that sense of charity to a gifted stranger,

open to their gatherings, these voluble bores,
these brilliant jeerers. Friends are a danger,

proud of the tribal subtleties of their
suffering, its knot of meaning, of blood on the street

for an idea, their pain is privilege, a clear
tradition, proud in triumph, prouder in defeat,

for which they have made a language they share
in intellectual, odourless sweat.

Because they measure evil by the seasons, the clear
death of October, its massacre of leaves,

my monodic climate has no history. I hear
their bright applause for one another's lives.

My fault was ignorance of their History
and my contempt for it, they are my Old Masters,

sunlight and pastures, a tireless sea
with its one tense, one crest where the last was.

No scansion for the seasons, no epochs
for the fast scumbling surf, no dates

or decades for the salt-streaming rocks,
no spires or towers for the sailing frigates.

4

One sunrise I felt an ordinary
width of enlightenment in my motel,

at the Ramada Inn in Albany.
I was bent, writing, he was bent as well,

but in nineteenth-century St. Thomas
my body filled his pencilled silhouette

in arched Dronningens Gade, my trousers
rolled to the calves, in a sisal hat at the market

which I now tip in my acknowledgement
to him and Mr. Melbye. I'll be born

a hundred years later, but we're both bent
over this paper; I am being drawn,

anonymous as my own ancestor,
my Africa erased, if not his France,

the cobbled sunlit street with a dirt floor
and a quick sketch my one inheritance.

Then one noon where acacias shade the beach
I saw the parody of Tiepolo's hound

in the short salt grass, requiring no research,
but something still unpainted, on its own ground.

I had seen wolfhounds straining on the leash,
their haunches taut on tapestries of Spring;

now I had found, whose azure was a beach,
this tottering, abandoned, houseless thing.

A starved pup trembling by the hard sea,
far from the back yards of a village street.

She cried out in compassion. This was not the
cosseted lapdog in its satin seat,

not even Goya's mutt peering from a fissure
of that infernal chasm in the Prado,

but one that shook with local terror, unsure
of everything, even its shadow.

Its swollen belly was shivering from the heat
of starvation; she moaned and picked it up,

this was the mongrel's heir, not in a great
fresco, but bastardy, abandonment, and hope

and love enough perhaps to help it live
like all its breed, and charity, and care,

we set it down in the village to survive
like all my ancestry. The hound was here.

(XXIII)

1

Teaching in St. Thomas, I had never sought it out,
the Synagogue of Blessing and Peace and Loving Deeds;

in the tourist streets I never gave a thought
to the lost shops that were Dronningens Gade's.

Liners whitened the hectic port, as always,
with the exact, vivid banality

of its postcards; its sunlit stone alleys
hid the lost *shul* of Charlotte Amalie

but along hot shadowed roads frothing with trees
that led to the steep college, you saw

those customary pastorals of the Antilles,
yards and rust fences that he learnt to draw.

I passed, climbing the hot hill to the college,
him and Fitz Melbye sketching in the shade.

I stopped. I heard their charcoals scratch the page
and their light laughter, but not what they said.

I felt a line enclose my lineaments
and those of other shapes around me too,

a bare dirt yard stacked with old implements,
its patterned leaves, cross-hatched, and as the view

grew backwards quickly, I grew back as well,
my clothes were lighter and my stance as frozen

as the pencilled branches of an immortelle.
I shrank into the posture they had chosen,

and felt, in barefoot weightlessness, that choice
transparently defined, straw hat, white cotton

fabric, drawn with a withdrawn voice,
knowing that I, not it, would be forgotten,

keeping my position as a model does,
a young slave, mixed and newly manumitted

last century and a half in old St. Thomas,
my figure now emerging, and it said:

"I and my kind move and not move; your drawing
is edged with a kindness my own lines contain,

but yours may just be love of your own calling
and not for us, since sunshine softens pain,

and we seem painless here, or the marketplace
where I discern myself among its figures,

placid adornments, models of the race.
Mission-accomplished, exile-humming niggers

by a bay's harp, in pencil-shaded yards,
here for your practice; but do not leave us here,

for cities where our voices have no words."
Our figures muttered, but he could not hear,

and to this day they still receive no answer,
even while I scolded his fast-shadowed hand.

"We lost our roots as yours were far Braganza,
but this is our new world, of reeds and sand."

Both kept on drawing, and the sketch each made
that leafy afternoon was left unsigned,

holding my body while my spirit strayed
in catalogues, where I can never find

its exact apparition, as I have not found,
though I am sure I saw it, Tiepolo's

or Paolo Veronese's spectral hound,
I hide in white among white cotton Negroes.

I said, "You could have been our pioneer.
Treacherous Gauguin judged you a second-rater.

Yours could have been his archipelago, where
hues are primal, red trees, green shade, blue water."

He said, "My history veins backwards
to the black soil of my birthplace, whose trees

are a hallowed forest; its leaf-words
uttering the language of my ancestors,

then, for ringed centuries, a helpless dimming
of distance made both bark and language fade

to an alphabet of bats and swallows skimming
the twilight gables of Dronningens Gade."

The ground doves brood and strut, a swallow calls
from crusted eaves, "Adieu, Monsieur Gauguin";

the placid afternoons of his pastorals
once he changed islands; both began again,

one on the Ile de Paris's moss-blackened walls
with barges creasing the mud-coloured Seine,

the other near Tahiti's waterfalls
and flower-haired women in their foaming basin.

Are all the paintings then falsifications
of his real origins, was his island betrayed?

Instead of linden walks and railway stations,
our palms and windmills? Think what he would have made

(but how could he, what colour was his Muse,
and what was there to paint except black skins?)

of flame trees in the fields of Santa Cruz;
others took root and stood the difference,

and some even achieved a gratitude
beyond their dislocation, saw what was given

and seized it with possessed delight, made good
from an infernal, disease-riddled heaven,

and let the ship go, trailing its red banner
out of their harbour, like *The Téméraire*.

St. Thomas stays unpainted, every savannah
trails its flame tree that fades. This is not fair.

3

Out of the open window, the tall palms dream
of Zion, the thick clouds graze like sheep,

"If I forget thee . . ." Children share childhood. See him,
one oven-hot afternoon when parents sleep,

stretched out on a straw carpet, an innocent
studying the freight train of a millipede

before the world into which we are sent
stings with each poisonous and different creed.

He saw frigates veer over a smoky hill,
all that, regenerate, recurs; he would have seen

in flower beds a hummingbird's soundless drill
with electric wings, its emerald machine

that darts as soon as it settles, a windmill's
vanes grind to a halt with slavery, the sign

of the season changing on scorched hills
a rainbow's fury, the rain's trawling seine.

He woke, like us, to dew. He watched voracious
caterpillars of rain nibble the horizon,

the sun-dried tamarinds, rusting acacias
grown brittle as firewood for August's oven,

saw puffs of cloud from the fort's rusted cannon,
regiments of slaughtered flowers at the root

of cedars whose huge shade contracts at noon,
smelled earth's scorched iron in the autumnal drought.

Surely he recalled how the remorseless March
sun scorched the hills, the consoling verandahs,

the family afternoons on the fretwork porch
in the infinity of Antillean Sundays,

to the soft bellows of a butterfly's wings,
the folded Bible of a velvet moth,

THE SWIMMER, 1995
Watercolour on paper, 14″ x 19″

a swaying canna lily's bell that brings
a hymn of black flies to a tablecloth.

Sea-wires on the ceiling, he watched them once,
from the languor of mosquito nets, lying down,

paralysed by floating afternoons,
the sea, past scorching roofs, a leaden cauldron.

Seasons and paintings cross, reversible,
Hobbema's, the shade-crossed casuarina walk,

the surf foams in apple orchards, cedars talk
poplar, and autumn claims the hills of April.

Grenade sugar-apples, cannonball calabash,
the first breeze and the cool of coming rain

from moaning ground doves, the burnt smell of bush,
the flecks of sea beyond a sugar mill's ruin,

decrepit doors in back yards blowing smoke,
a black pup nosing puddles by a yam fence,

from a dog to the Doge's Palace, drains that mock,
with gliding leaves and reeds, aureate Venice.

Once, near Dinard, a Roman aqueduct
soaring in sea mist, a rook shipped its oars,

in a homecoming glide, with wings it tucked
like brushes that lie crossed after Pontoise.

4

These couplets climb the pillared sanctum
of invitation to Salon, Academy,

its lectern for the elect. I thank them
for helping me to cross a treacherous sea

to find a marble hound. Mutely pleading
outside is a black mongrel; I examine a small

bas-relief that shows a wolfhound leading
a straining huntress. Well, it is fall,

so the season flares and fades, a reading,
an opening, a lavish catalogue

of homage to Tiepolo, gossip, breeding.
I think of reeking fish and a black dog.

(**XXIV**)

1

The sunrise, brightening the roof's cold slate,
lifted the pigeons from Madrid, they'd rise,

then settle on the eaves, where they would wait
with brooding murmurs; summer's deepening skies

were thick with galleons, even far Braganza
from which the Pissarros sailed for paradise.

Fine and fresh mornings. Doe-eyed Esperanza,
José Antonio, pavements hosed till the sun

rattled café grids open, stanza by stanza,
this was his light, this where his sight began.

Spring in Saarbrücken, laburnum-yellow words
in a choked canal, the mesmerising stones

of Venice, the wake roiling backwards
from a firing vaporetto, Roberta's cheekbones,

sharp as the elbow of a road in Sicily,
maps made in the heart, its cherished places

as in mild Mantua, Mayrah and Luigi,
at our own open feast, their sunstruck faces.

Pastoral gusts herded far flocks of cloud
above the walls of ancient Alcalá;

the light had substance; a still life that could
share with the ham and bread the taste of colour.

Storks, odd and gangly, nested in the tower
of the university; the light's soft argument

persuaded buildings with its gentle power
of definition in arches and pavement.

Tiepolo saw this. Perhaps his shadow slid
over these cobbled alleys where Cervantes

lived once. It was not far from Madrid.
In the Aranjuez altarpieces he paints

his last great canvases, he never saw again
the children he left behind, nor the wife

who bore them; at dusk the light of Spain
was like his ceilings, fading with his life.

The bells clanged punishingly from the convent;
by now it must have deafened all the nuns

and maddened its local scrivener, who went
next to his skeletal knight on expeditions,

shaking his head, muttering with Sancho Panza,
past windmills you can still see on the road;

the cloud-flocks moving, shadowing far Braganza
in Portugal, in the one light they shared.

A light exchanged, its history a surrender
to what was undeniable in place and name,

a spectral empire to which every defender
of our primal islands yielded with a slow shame.

Under the sky's rotunda I had found
in all this wealth of time, its power, its feast,

its clamorous bells, wandering like a hound,
made homeless as those distances increased

that left me emptiness as an inheritance
except the eyes of Esperanza and the laughter

of José Antonio. In Alcalá, in France,
I had no shadow, no before and after.

There lies, in that far light, a difference
hallowed by age, like wine, and cured like cheese;

on the streets of Spain, the watery doors of Venice,
the casuarinas cast long memories.

2

Real counties opened from that small blue book
I cherished: *The English Topographical Draughtsmen*,

turning page after page, now I would look
at what my father never saw, craftsmen

made real by names and counties, high clouds
over the counties, the copses and meadows

with posing cows, the illustrations closed
and camphored in the bookcase of our house.

I watched the mist with an old innocence
of wonder as he did, both island boys,

when steam smothered the small streets of Louveciennes
and seized Pontoise, cannon smoke without noise.

Fog I first learnt in Sussex, where it hovered
over the dissolving Downs, thickening the yard

through which trees peered and hedges were covered
by the smoking county, until its cataract barred

vision entirely. I knew its history here,
in films and novels, opaque conspirator.

On the ancient road we had startled a hare
who melted in it, a raindrop in water.

In the shrouded distance the barking of a dog
would carry over the shrouding copses, over

old words emerging from their roots, fen, bog,
and weald, but no fox leapt from cover,

no scarlet hunters vaulting from a pub print
over bowed hedges, a brass horn hallooing;

England became its art, no different,
except for the hound. I was the one pursuing.

Where a grassed hillock surged towards a copse,
the word "broom" brandished itself, and there

an orotund oak, majestic in collapse,
exhausted that old metaphor of empire,

but I claimed nothing. Not from this landscape,
the ragged hedges opening Warwickshire,

not in my father's name, those fields of rape,
not even that blue patch where the sun was higher

over the sodden fields. Nothing ancestral
that I could see, nothing from the spire

of piercing Coventry. I heard the small
echoes in the skull's nave, an island choir,

responses carried in the polite noise
of rain beading the windows of the car,

as if this was the drizzle of Pontoise—
wires of rain encaging the familiar.

Nothing blood-recollected in the soil
of watercolour country, slopes with cows,

a broken castle, unlike his: an oil
of silvery willows on the flashing Oise.

3

I looked beyond the tarmac. A bright field.
Late horizontal afternoon. Light, south

of the island. My grief unhealed
by the sacral egrets at a river's mouth

or the great geese crossing through my face
in the car window. I could see the foam

of Maria Island chafing at its base
and shadow-widowed sand. Four months from home.

I saw this promontory fringed with grass,
tall, bleached-white grass, the pennons of the drought

more straw than shoots. Then I knew where it was:
the blithely running sea around Vieux-Fort,

the low cliffs that abruptly end in cactus,
in the agave's viridian detonations,

when we first painted and our shadows tracked us
up stone-loose paths towards the Atlantic's patience.

In the cold morning reeds disconsolate geese,
their great wings hammering the marsh-light silver,

launched their far squadrons in convulsive V's
south, south like arrows from the rushes' quiver!

Meadows and spires resumed from sinuous trains
in widening sunlight, while catarrhal geese

kept honking south, leaving brown mountains
jagged with ice, hard lakes, and iron trees.

Brown Italy, and azure Adriatic
of *faux-châteaux*, the mountains speckled ochre,

the snowline, and the shelving forests thick
as libraries, homesick for my acre,

for the green crests of Charlotte Amalie,
the yellow synagogue so far from Braganza,

for a mongrel in the shadows of an alley
on an island Sunday, a park's sunlit stanza.

4

Fall; and a cool blonde crosses Christopher—
braid coronet, skin colour: Veronese.

I stare. A brace of white hounds bolt from her
unleashed, to foam around Actaeon's knees.

In golden light, that *noli tangere*
which keeps its frame and distance on a street,

that utterance which has no words to say
as if it were a fresco will repeat

an old division. There's such a busy busy
biography between her and her clothes

(though less than those brocades of Veronese);
I have added more wolfhounds than Tiepolo's.

Hunched in its outline, the beast turned snarling
with one look from the wall, in recognition.

Then, flagging a leaf-yellow cab, my darling
yanked its neck with her hand, then they were gone.

From my tired taxi, rattling towards Kennedy,
the last defiant maples were on fire;

along a verge skeletal trees stood ready
for the thin winter sun, their usual fare.

The maple pyres, not merely fallen but curled
in their decrepitude, were bearing me

from autumn's acclamation of a world
flashing with its deciduous poetry,

and that blurred tapestry of incoherence
that passed for painting, from the age itself.

So many leaves blown from that stricken fence
of friends that have become spines on a shelf!

And then I turned and saw, racing the taxi,
through crossed twigs, billboards, a shrouding underpass,

with stalled, jerking traffic, the shadowy ecstasy
of a black mongrel loping behind glass.

1

I suppose I should have told you about Louveciennes
and the other villages where he took a house

with his brood of seven, shown where this street ends
and that lane forks, those walks of a Pontoise

I have never seen except as his accompanying
shadow on leaf-glued autumn pavements, or

crunching bright piebald snow, but I kept seeing
things through his eyes: a gate, a rusted door,

since all our radiant bush, a road, a hill
with torches of pouis, a shade-stayed stream

made joy recede to memory, our provincial
palms, bowing, withdraw before his dream,

as History's distance shrank a crescent fringe
of rustling yellow fronds on a white shore,

a house, a harbour with its mountain range
to a dot named by its cartographer—

the name longer than the dot. In Trinidad
there was one painter, the Frenchman Cazabon,

whose embalmed *paysages* were all we had,
our mongrel culture gnawing its one bone.

Cazabon and Pissarro; the first is ours,
the second found the prism that was Paris,

rooted in France, his dark-soiled ancestors;
no matter, cherish the conviction their work carries.

2

Affliction: inflammation of the eyes
that often stops him painting. The tears run,

but older than tears is the paralysis
of doubt, unchanged from when he first began,

since man is a small island who contains
cisterns of sorrow, and drought that absence dries,

and doubt; St. Thomas hazing as it rains
and love, the mist-bow bent on paradise.

In his life's dusk, though hand and eye grow weary,
his concentration strengthens in its skill,

some critics think his work is ordinary,
but the ordinary is the miracle.

Ordinary love and ordinary death,
ordinary suffering, ordinary birth,

the ordinary couplets of our breath,
ordinary heaven, ordinary earth.

To watch the moving sea, heavy and silver
on a mid-August afternoon, then turn

his catalogue of views of the great river
dragging its barges, so little time to learn,

you are taken there, though, by his brush's
delicate frenzy, by all his tenderness

even for winter scenes, when the snow hushes
the rasping surface and a boulevard's noise.

My Paris comes out of his canvases
not from a map, and perhaps, even better

than Paris itself; they fill these verses
with their own light, their walks, their weather

that will outlast me as they outlast him,
their hustling crowds, their carriages in strokes,

fresh, fast, and trembling, as in a film
where wheels stop and run backwards, silver spokes

of drizzle down this boulevard, that park
where I can gaze at leisure, taking time

to loiter at each stroke, at the faint arc
of a white bridge; so modest, so sublime!

3

Paint a true street in Anse La Raye, Choiseul,
the roasting asphalt, the bleached galvanise roofs

grooved like these lines, paint the dark heat as well
inside the canted shacks, do the blurred hooves

of a boy whooping a white mare near a lagoon
for gone Gauguin, paint the violet bruise

of reef under water wiry at noon,
paint the cathedral's solace, the canoes

resting in the almonds, always the same
canoes resting under the almonds, and next you could

paint the thick flowers too poor to have a name,
that couple entering a shading wood

for something no longer your business,
mix the light's colour with that pliant knife

that is your plasterer's trowel. It would be nice
to do this in deep gratitude for your life,

just as its hallelujahs praise their giver
the chalk-white chapel portals of La Fargue

before la Rivière Doreé, the sun-gilt river,
whose missal shallows recite your epilogue.

4

Our tribes were shaken like seeds from a sieve.
Our dialects, rooted, forced their own utterance,

and what were we without the slow belief
in our own nature? Not Guinea, not Provence.

And yet so many fled, so many lost
to the magnetic spires of cities, not the cedars,

as if a black pup turned into the ghost
of the white hound, but a search that will lead us

where we began: to islands, not the busy
but unchanged patronage of the empire's centre,

guests at the roaring feast of Veronese,
or Tiepolo's Moors, where once we could not enter.

Camille Pissarro must have heard the noise
of loss-lamenting slaves, and if he did,

they tremble in the poplars of Pontoise,
the trembling, elegiac tongues he painted.

Swivel the easel down, drill it in sand,
then tighten the canvas against vaps of wind,

straddle the stool, reach for the brush with one hand,
then pour the oil in trembling sacrament.

There is another book that is the shadow
of my hand on this sunlit page, the one

I have tried hard to write, but let this do;
let gratitude redeem what lies undone.

(XXVI)

1

The swallows flit in immortality,
moving yet motionless on the canvas roofs,

like signatures, memorials to his city,
swifter than strokes along a ledger's proofs

as when the V's of gulls skimmed the capped harbour,
lifting their cries above Dronningens Street,

and creaking canvas sails furled in their labour
of journeys finished in the Sunday heat.

Dusk in the islands. Gusts of swallows wheeling
over Paris and the furrows of Pontoise,

in couplets under a Tiepolo ceiling.
He enters the window frame. His gaze is yours.

Primed canvas, steaming mirror, this white page
where a drawing emerges. His portrait sighs

from a white fog. Pissarro in old age,
as we stand doubled in each other's eyes.

To endure affliction with no affection gone
seems to have been the settlement in those eyes,

whose lenses catch a glinting winter sun
on mansards and the rigid smoke of chimneys.

It is one of the mildest winters on record.
His glasses flash across the spray-burst beard,

a true timidity of disregard
from the halo of the bohemian beret.

Perhaps he wears it indoors from the cold,
the eyes are sunken, but their stare no sadder

under the arched brows than when the family strolled
the Danish stonework of Dronningens Gade;

the skeptic turned to a Sephardic sage,
rabbinical in his fragility,

since the snow's rapid strokes whitened a page
of canvas and we lost him to a city.

If the surf of apple orchards could be heard,
its murmur would come through this foaming page

where he chats with Cézanne in a flecked beard,
hat, boots, and staff; his palmer's pilgrimage.

Meanwhile, the palms, in their eternal summers,
rustling like children's lessons in the heat,

bring the occasional pilgrim to St. Thomas
to find the synagogue on its small street.

The soul is indivisible as air.
Supposedly, all things become a dream,

but we, as moving trees, must root somewhere,
and there our separation shows its seam,

in our attachment to the nurturing place
of earth, a buried string, a chattering stream

or still lagoon that holds our fading face,
that wrinkles from the egret's rising scream.

Time takes one hand and helps us up the stair,
Time draws the shades down on our clouding eyes;

they go together, painting and white hair,
a sea rock streaming, or skeined cirrus skies,

a mottled scalp of sun-receding snow
in piebald patches on a furrowed path,

in landscapes with no tenses, views that know
that now, as always, light is all we have.

Three years into the century, his sight
has failed, he paints from an open window

overlooking the street. One starry night
the vigil candles end. Dawn is his widow.

His brushes rest. Canvas and tombstone whiten.
Mattock and chisel hyphenate his fame.

The lindens flutter. The parentheses tighten
(and enclose Paris in Pissarro's name).

Help me to crease the pleats of an emerald sleeve
Giambattista Tiepolo, Paolo Veronese,

an idling wrist, the light through a cloud's sieve,
Camille Pissarro, on our beaches the breezy

light over our bays, help me to begin
when I set out again, at sixty-nine,

for the sacred villages. Dole out, in each tin,
clear linseed and redemptive turpentine.

I shall finish in a place whose only power
is the exploding spray along its coast,

its rotting asphalt and cantankerous poor
numb beyond resignation and its cost,

and I endure the gorgonizing glare
and toothless bitterness of destitution,

and hard soles scraping on a half-baked square,
though in his own day he saw no solution

except escape, as sprats race undersea
from a dividing shadow. What was his sin?

Where there's no trust there is no treachery.
The nets sag from black poles against the sun.

This is my peace, my salt, exulting acre:
there is no more Exodus, this is my Zion,

whose couplets race the furrowing wind, their maker,
with those homecoming sails on the horizon.

3

A dog barks in an unchanged neighbourhood,
Petit Valley marks the pilgrimage I have made,

its clouds spread in a linen gratitude
of fruit in a bowl, a pomme-arac's lilac shade,

and what lights the mind around sunlit corners
of Chumamonka Avenue's scorching asphalt

is a remembered happiness, now one as
grateful for the pardon of a deep fault;

passing thorns of forgiving bougainvillea,
raw scars on the old hill as age enjoys

the frames of a lost life again familiar—
Morne Coco, or the poplars of Pontoise.

For shaded corners of the Santa Cruz road
where sometimes you see horses through the trunks,

their hides reddish brown, umber, tan, coloured
like the trunks. For leaves and horses, thanks.

4

Let this page catch the last light on Becune Point,
lengthen the arched shadows of Charlotte Amalie,

to a prayer's curling smoke, and brass anoint
the branched menorah of a frangipani,

as the lights in the shacks bud orange across the Morne,
and are pillared in the black harbour. Stars fly close

as sparks, and the houses catch with bulb and lampion
to the Virgin, Veronese's and Tiepolo's.

Soon, against the smoky hillsides of Santa Cruz,
dusk will ignite the wicks of the immortelle,

parrots will clatter from the trees with raucous news
of the coming night, and the first star will settle.

Then all the sorrows that lay heavily on us,
the repeated failures, the botched trepidations

will pass like the lights on bridges at village corners
where shadows crouch under pierced constellations

whose name they have never learnt, as a sickle glow
rises over bamboos that repeat the round

of the charted stars, the Archer, aiming his bow,
the Bear, and the studded collar of Tiepolo's hound.